# A Journey with Omar Khayaam

**Wes Jamroz**

Troubadour Publications

# A Journey with Omar Khayaam

Editing:            *Dominique Hugon, Patrick Barnard*
Cover design:       *Sandra Viscuso*
Cover illustration: *"The wine's bouquet"* by *Sandra Viscuso*

Montreal, QC, Canada

TroubadourPubs@aol.com
http://www.troubadourpublications

ISBN: 978-1-928060-07-9

You will have to undergo experiences, which we call "journeys," which may or may not involve conventional travel, to make it possible for you to recognise truth when you find it.

*(Journeys with a Sufi Master*, by H.B.M. Dervish)

# A Note on Texts

The 111 quatrains and their arrangement are quoted from Omar Ali-Shah's translation *The Authentic Rubaiyyat of Omar Khayaam* (IDSI, 1993)

The excerpts from Rumi's *Mathnawi* are extracted by the author from Reynold A. Nicholson's translation *The Mathnawi of Jalaluddin Rumi* (E.J. W. Gibb Memorial, 1926)

The quotations of Shakespeare's plays and sonnets are from *The Riverside Shakespeare* (Second Edition, 1997)

# Table of Contents

# INTRODUCTION

More than 2,000 books and articles have been written about Omar Khayaam. Omar Khayaam[1] was a distinguished mathematician, astronomer, and a poet. As a mathematician, he is most notable for his work on the classification and solution of cubic equations. As an astronomer, he designed the Persian calendar which proved to be more accurate than that proposed five centuries later by Pope Gregory XIII. He became known as a poet through his *Rubaiyyat*, a collection of poems written in the form of quatrains.

The collections of Khayaam's quatrains have grown immensely, from 158 quatrains in the manuscript dated 1460 that is held at the Bodleian Library at Oxford to 1,955 quatrains listed by Swami Govinda Tirtha in his book *The Nectar of Grace*.[2] In recent years, some scholars embarked on the challenging task of sorting out the grains from the chaff, i.e., identifying the quatrains that, most probably, were written by Omar Khayaam. For example, Ali Dashti, an Iranian writer, attempted to identify the authentic verses by building a synthetic portrait of Khayaam, including his personality, beliefs, philosophy, his likes and dislikes. In his book *In Search of Omar Khayyam*, Dashti used this portrait to select quatrains that according to his method were unquestionably written by Khayaam.[3] A reviewer of Dashti's book has observed that:

---

[1] Some authors transliterated the name of *Khayaam* as *Khayyam*.

[2] *The Nectar of Grace*, Swami Govinda Tirtha (1941; republished by Oxford City Press in 2010).

[3] *In Search of Omar Khayyam*, Ali Dashti (Routledge, 1971; originally published in Iran in 1966).

If Omar Khayyam was an ordinary poet, i.e., belonging to the same rank as, for example, Edward Fitzgerald -the very famous transmogrifier of Khayyam's poetry- then such a method might be somewhat correct. But if Omar Khayyam's poetry is part of the so-called spiritual technology, then such a method is absolutely useless. His poetry is a deeply philosophic set rather than an autobiographic outpouring. Let's recall that such poets as Rumi, Saadi, and Hafiz wrote their poetry because this was the most effective way to transmit specific evolutionary concepts and ideas ahead of their actual realization. In this way the human mind could be prepared for their correct assimilation. Such an impact contained in the poetry is not detectable in a poet's personality, beliefs, philosophy, or way of behaviour. Therefore, trying to identify traces of such impact in fragmented documents about a person is as fruitless as, to quote Rumi, "trying to reach the milk by way of the cheese."[4]

Omar Khayaam belonged to a school which claims that within mankind there is a latent element that provides the means of attaining to true reality. Through the activation of this element man may overcome the limitations of physical existence and fulfill his ultimate evolutionary function. This school has been known as the science of Divine Wisdom. It is said that the school originated from somewhere beyond our usual time-space conception. This science offers the methodology and techniques needed to sensitize the human mind and prepare it for experiences which cannot be transmitted by scholastic methods. Such experiences may be induced by establishing a bond between a guide and his pupil. Through this bond a guide may expose his pupil to the currently projected evolutionary matrix of an advanced human mind. The literary materials produced by the school contain preparatory impacts needed for the effective assimilation of the matrix. These impacts work in such a way as to guide and, if necessary, rectify any

---

[4] Amazon.com: *In Search of Omar Khayyam*, a review by Roman Paget (Sept. 7, 2016).

deviation from the predestined course of the human evolutionary path. The evolutionary matrix changes as soon as it is effectively assimilated by a select group of people in a given community. Then an updated matrix in its higher order form is projected and a new true poet arrives on the scene. Therefore, the literary materials produced by the school belong to their own time, place and environment.

The true poets introduce new allegorical illustrations and in so doing enable the literary materials to continue a dynamic function. As in the waves-of-the-sea metaphor, the evolutionary impact is constantly renewed by successive true poets. It is in this manner that man is guided along his evolutionary path.

Historically, Omar Khayaam was the first in a line of poets that included Sanai, Attar, Rumi, Saadi, Hafiz, Jami. Khayaam, before Rumi, used the same imagery of the bezel of a ring to describe the function of his poetry: "This circle of the universe resemble a ring/Unquestionably we are the signet engraved on its bezel."[5] Recently, it has been demonstrated that Shakespeare belonged to this same school of true poets.[6]

We may look at Khayaam's, Rumi's and Shakespeare's writings as the illustrations of three consecutive stages of man's evolutionary progress. Khayaam lived in 11th century Persia. Khayaam's *Rubaiyyat* is a reflection on man's spiritual state at that time in that specific community. Rumi lived in the 13th century Sultanate of Rum (in today's Turkey). His writings are a symbolic representation of the evolutionary matrix projected at that time in that specific geographical area. Shakespeare's plays and his sonnets are based on the evolutionary matrix that was projected in 16th century England.

[5] Khayaam's quatrain #340 quoted by Prof. Nicholson in *Divan-e Shams-e Tabrizi*, Jalaluddin Rumi (Cambridge University Press, 1898; republished by Ibex Publishers in 2016).
[6] *Shakespeare's Elephant in Darkest England*, W. Jamroz (Troubadour Publications, 2016).

Each of them describes specific stages of the spiritual journey which reveal the mysteries of the hidden worlds:

> From these stars, like inverted candles,
> From those blue awnings of the Sky
> Has come forth a wondrous people, so that
> The Mysteries may be revealed
> (*Divan-e Shams-e Tabrizi*[7])

Each of these poets described the evolutionary summit that was available to man at his time and his place. The following episode from the life of Abdul-Qadir of Gilan may serve as an illustration of the evolutionary nature of the spiritual teaching:

> Abdul-Qadir was asked by one of his disciples "Can you not give us power to improve the earth and the lot of the people of the earth?" He answered: "I will do better: I will give this power to your descendants, because as yet there is no hope of such improvement being made on a large enough scale. The devices do not yet exist. You shall be rewarded; and they shall have the reward of their efforts and of your aspiration."[8]

Abdul-Qadir died in 1166. He left a patched robe to be presented to a successor to his mandate who was to be born nearly four hundred years later. The robe was invested with the Sheikh Ahmed Faruqi of Sirhind. Ahmed Faruqi was a contemporary to Shakespeare. It was suggested that Ahmed Faruqi, "an Indian king," inspired Shakespeare's writings.[9]

By charting the stages of the evolutionary development of the human mind presented in Khayaam's, Rumi's and Shakespeare's writings, it is possible to get a measure of the progress achieved

---

[7] *Divan-e Shams-e Tabrizi*, Jalaluddin Rumi (Translated by R.A. Nicholson, Cambridge University Press, 1898; republished by Ibex Publishers in 2016).
[8] *Tales of the Dervishes*, Idries Shah (Octagon Press, 1967).
[9] See Note #6.

between the 11th and 17th centuries. In other words, their writings symbolically reflect three points along the curve representing the evolutionary growth of humanity.

According to the science of Divine Wisdom, the human inner being consists of three centres or manifest faculties: self, heart, and intellect. Survival as well as the desire for and the pursuit of pleasure, ambitions, self-importance and greed - all these are the attributes of the self faculty.

Entertaining feelings of love and hatred, showing bravery or cowardice, forming an intention and carrying out a particular action - these are the characteristics of the heart faculty.

Understanding and knowledge, the capacity to perceive, to recollect things of the past and plan for things of the future - these are the qualities that are attributed to the intellect faculty.

The intellect and the heart faculties are not homogenous. They consist of a multi-layered inner structure. This inner structure may be unfolded, layer-by-layer, through a purification process. During the purification process, the inner layers of the intellect or the heart are activated. These inner layers are known as special or subtle faculties.

Khayyam indicated that real knowledge is gained through the purification of the intellect faculty. The purification of the intellect is the product of experience and not of formal learning. Khayaam referred to such an inspirational experience as *drunkenness*. Consequently, the main theme of his *Rubaiyyat* is *wine*, which he uses as a metaphor for a purifying impact that removes the ordinary intellect veils. In this way, subtle layers of the intellect may be activated.

Sir John Falstaff in Shakespeare's *Henry IV* gives a compelling description of the purifying effect of wine ("sherries") on the ordinary intellect ("brain"):

> A good sherris-sack hath a twofold operation in it. It ascends me into the brain; dries me there all the foolish and dull and curdy vapours which environ it; makes it apprehensive, quick, forgetive, full of nimble, fiery and delectable shapes, which, deliver'd o'er to the voice, the tongue, which is the birth, becomes excellent wit. ...
> (*Henry IV, part 2, IV.3*)

Falstaff seems to echo Khayaam's theme by saying that *non-drinkers* are all generally foolish and dull. He explains that wine is capable of drying out all the foolish and dull fogs that clog up the brain. This makes the brain sharp and inventive, full of fiery and beautiful ideas. In other words, it is this sort of *wine* which activates subtle layers of the intellect.

After unveiling the subtle layers of the intellect, the next stage of the process aims at the activation of subtle layers of the heart faculty. In his monologue, Falstaff continues the symbolic description of the process:

> ... The second property of your excellent sherris is the warming of the blood; which before (cold and settled) left the liver white and pale, which is the badge of pusillanimity and cowardice; but the sherris warms it, and makes it course from the inwards to the parts' extreme. It illumineth the face, which as a beacon gives warning to all the rest of this little kingdom, man, to arm, and then the vital commoners and inland petty spirits muster me all to their captain, the heart, who great and puffed up with this retinue, doth any deed of courage; and this valour comes of sherris.
> (*Henry IV, part 2, IV.3*)

The second effect of wine is purifying the heart. Wine warms the blood. Then blood gathers together all the internal organs behind the heart, their captain. The heart is strengthened by *drunkenness*. This transforms a coward into a courageous one. Wine is what sets the new valor in motion. This new ability is a symbolic mark of activated subtle layers of the heart faculty.

The subtle faculties, i.e., inner layers of the human mind, are those "devices" that were not activated yet at a large enough scale at the time of Abdul-Qadir. The subtle faculties together with the ordinary intellect and heart faculties form an inner being, an inner structure of the human mind. Falstaff refers to this inner structure as "this little kingdom." The gradual development of this inner structure is the driving force of human evolution and the purpose of human existence.

After the activation of the subtle faculties of the intellect and the heart, "this little kingdom" needs to be transmuted into a new organ of perception. It is this organ that allows the human mind to overcome the limitation of physical existence. This is done by uniting the newly activated subtle faculties. Before they can be united, these faculties have to be harmonized with the currently projected evolutionary matrix. *Love* acts as the agent needed to accomplish this particular stage of the process. But this is not ordinary sensual or emotional love which simply beautifies existence; this is *love* which transforms existence. This stage of the process was allegorically illustrated by Rumi as a lover and his beloved. The lover represents "this little kingdom." His beloved is an impulse of evolutionary impact. By absorbing this impact, the lover's selfish desires and attachments are consumed by the flames of *love*; the subtle faculties are united and transmuted into a new organ of perception. The lover's existence is transformed into another form of life: a New Man is born.

Shakespeare used his plays to describe the evolutionary history of western society; each of his plays illustrates a particular episode of the evolutionary process. His characters represent these various ordinary and latent faculties of the mind. Duke Orsino, a character that appears in Shakespeare's *Twelfth Night*, refers to the new organ of perception as "one self king." "Liver, brain, and heart" symbolically indicate the self faculty, the intellect faculty and the heart faculty, respectively. The self king appears when love ("the rich golden shaft") kills all raw emotions and attachments ("the flock of all affections"):

> How will she love when the rich golden shaft
> Hath kill'd the flock of all affections else
> That live in her; when liver, brain and heart,
> These sovereign thrones, are all supplied, and fill'd
> Her sweet perfections with one self king!
> (*Twelfth Night*, I.1)

At the time of Shakespeare, an advanced methodology was introduced, whereby a number of the subtle faculties could be activated simultaneously. In this way, the process of spiritual transmutation could be greatly accelerated. Symbolically, this advanced methodology is illustrated as four couples of lovers who are to be married at the same place and at the same time. In other words, Rumi's "lover" is split into four lovers. Two lovers indicate latent faculties of the intellect; the other two represent latent faculties of the heart. Their beloveds are the corresponding evolutionary impulses. Together they signify the operating evolutionary matrix that takes the form of "eight," a form capable of holding "true contents." Such a symbolic "eight" (*octagon*) is formed at the conclusion of Shakespeare's play *As You Like It*, when Hymen, the god of marriage, comments:

Here's eight that must take hands
To join in Hymen's bands,
    If truth holds true contents.
(*As You Like It*, V.4)

At this point, the previously used methods of spiritual technology
became obsolete and a new set of techniques was introduced. It is
in this context that Khayaam's, Rumi's and Shakespeare's writings
are examples of "that which is introduced into the domain of Time
will fall victim to the ravages of Time."[10]

In order to be functionally useful, any translation of these poets'
writings requires familiarity with the operating evolutionary matrix
at that time, so its organic elements can be extracted, preserved and
correctly embodied in the text. But it is not just a correct
translation that preserves the original impact. In the case of
Khayaam, equally important is the selection of the quatrains and
their arrangement. Only some of the original quatrains are
applicable to the current state of the human mind. There is also the
time factor. This material had to wait for a specific time to have a
constructive impact on the readers in the West. It is in this context
that the translation of *The Authentic Rubaiyyat* by Omar Ali-Shah is
of great interest.[11] Omar Ali-Shah selected 111 quatrains, which
according to him are "poetically the most important ones." Let's
recall that at the time of the publication of Omar Ali-Shah's
translation, i.e., in the second half of the 20th century, specific
references to the evolution of the human mind were being released
to the general public for the first time. These publications
coincided with the scientific discovery of the effects of
conditioning, brain-washing and attitude-engineering. These
approaches inhibit the proper development of the human mind.
Through wide-scale implementation of these novel approaches, the

---

[10] *The Way of the Sufi*, Idries Shah (Octagon Press, 1968).
[11] *The Authentic Rubaiyyat of Omar Khayaam*, translated by Omar Ali-Shah and
illustrated by Eugenio Zanetti (©1993 IDSI, Los Angeles).

inherent evolutionary potential of the human mind could be greatly disturbed. It was then that Khayaam's poems were administered as a corrective measure. The appearance of *The Authentic Rubaiyyat of Omar Khayaam* was a sign that a new phase of the evolutionary projection was being implemented. This new phase of the process was initiated within the secular context of Western society.

According to Omar Ali-Shah, Khayaam's spiritual guide was Sheikh Mawaffikuddin. It was this Sheikh who suggested to Khayaam that *wine* should be the theme of his poetry. It may be helpful to recall that Khayaam lived at the same time as Yusuf Hamadani (1048-1140), a head of the Masters of the Divine Wisdom (Khwajagan). Hamadani introduced several new techniques as vehicles for the transmission of the evolutionary impacts. One of them was the method called *conversation* between a guide and his disciple. *The Authentic Rubaiyyat* is a record of the conversations between Khayaam and his Guide.

Rumi also used *conversation* in his writings. According to Rumi's own account, his life completely changed when he met Shams of Tabriz, a wandering dervish. Rumi recognized in Shams his spiritual guide. Afterwards, Rumi was transformed from an accomplished preacher and jurist into the greatest poet of Persian literature. It was Shams who requested that Rumi should record his teaching. The collection of Rumi's sonnets entitled *Divan-e Shams-e Tabrizi* is a record of his conversations with Shams.[12]

Similarly, Shakespeare's sonnets are written as conversations with his guide. As in the case of Khayaam and Rumi, his guide completely changed Shakespeare's life. He pointed out to Shakespeare that he was wasting his time and talent on meaningless writings. Then he taught him what to write. He led him through a

---

[12] See Note #7 (Prof. Nicholson, the translator of *Divan-e Shams-e Tabrizi*, was the first among the scholars to recognize Rumi's influence on Shakespeare's writings. In his explanatory notes he observed that Rumi's thoughts, terms and concepts may be found in Shakespeare's sonnets and plays).

sequence of experiences that allowed him to start to perceive the true value of his talent and the way in which his talent could be of use to a greater purpose. This purpose was spelled out in the Dedication that accompanied the first published edition of the sonnets. In a slightly paraphrased version, the Dedication[13] may also serve as an introduction to *A Journey with Omar Khayaam*:

To the only Inspirer of the ensuing verses,
I wish any traveler who embarked upon this journey all the happiness and eternity promised by our immortal poet, the inspired adventurer who undertook the task of writing them,
The Guide

*A Journey with Omar Khayaam* is a commentary on Khayaam's quatrains. There are two voices in *The Authentic Rubaiyyat*. First we hear the Guide who announces the commencement of the journey (the quatrain #1). In the quatrain #2 Khayaam describes the mood which prevails among his companions gathered in a tavern. The Guide delivers his first counsel in the quatrains #3 - #6. Then we hear Khayyam's reaction to the Guide's appeal (the quatrain #7). What follows are exchanges of the Guide's counsels and the Poet's reactions. The Guide speaks with authority and understanding; he is confident and his counsels follow a precise developmental methodology. The poet, on the other hand, is unsteady, hesitant and still affected by his intellectual and emotional conditioning.

---

[13] In the original text, the Dedication was addressed to "Master W.H.", and it was signed by "T.T." The meaning of the letters W, H, and T may be decoded through the *abjad* system. (The *abjad* gives letters of the alphabet numerical meaning; hence a number of mystical values can be translated into a single word or a letter, and vice-versa.) In their numerical equivalence, the letters W and H indicate the first and the final stages of a spiritual journey, i.e., from *initiation* (W) to achieving *inner harmony* (H). This means that the dedication was addressed to *any traveler*, who has entered onto the path. The meaning of the letter T is *inner knowledge*. It applies to the custodians of the evolutionary process. In other words, the Dedication was signed by a Guide. Shakespeare used this coding method on a couple of occasions, indicating that his writings were based on a design containing a methodology of activation of the inner faculties of the mind.

Throughout *The Authentic Rubaiyyat*, the Guide delivers 12 counsels. By following Khayyam's experiences, we witness how the Poet struggles with his intellectual biases and worldly attachments. As he goes through the initial stages of his spiritual training, his perception gradually develops and expands.

Khayaam's experiences are presented using a number of symbols such as wine, Saki, rose, tavern, death. The symbols that Khayaam uses are neither fixed nor static. The same symbol may mean different things depending on the context in which it is applied. The *Saki*, for example, may mean the Guide. At other times, the Saki denotes a disciple or it may indicate an actual person fulfilling a cupbearer's function. Sometimes, the Saki is used as an impersonal abstraction on which to hang a verse. Therefore, there is no such thing as a glossary of Khayaam's symbols. The same symbolic illustrations were used by Rumi and Shakespeare. Rumi and Shakespeare are from the same school of thought as Khayaam's; their writings are based on the same design. Therefore, quotes from Rumi and Shakespeare have been used in *A Journey with Omar Khayaam* to elucidate some of Khayaam's verses.

## The Drink of the Immortals

According to a mystical legend, the Saki (Cup-bearer) was to serve God every day with a cup of wine. Every morning, the cup would be replenished with wine only if the Saki had properly discharged his daily responsibilities and duties. On the fortieth morning of his impeccable service, the Saki was presented with a cup of the Drink of the Immortals. This legend inspired many tales about the challenges that a hero has to undertake in order to fulfil his heart's desire.

The opening quatrain of Omar Khayaam's *Rubaiyyat* contains a reference to this legend. The Sun, Day's regal Host, is replenishing his jug:

1

> While Dawn, Day's herald straddling the whole sky,
> Offers the drowsy world a toast 'To Wine',
> The Sun spills early gold on city roofs -
> Day's regal Host, replenishing his jug.

The Sun represents a spiritual guide. The appearance of a guide announces a new *Day*. The new Day brings new promises and challenges. It provides men with an opportunity to refill their *cups* by discharging correctly their duties and responsibilities. It is a very special moment. Sometimes it is referred to as a *forceful occasion*, whereby the time, the place, the presence of certain people and the overall environment are correctly aligned for an effective fulfilment of the evolutionary potential.

Shams of Tabriz (Sun of Tabriz), the spiritual guide of Rumi, used a similar imagery when comparing himself to the Sun:

> Mawlana [Rumi] is the moonlight.
> Eyes do not reach the sunlight of my existence,
> but they do reach the moon.
> Because of the extreme radiance and brightness of the sun,
> eyes do not have the capacity for it.
> Even that moon will not reach the sun, unless perhaps the sun
> reaches the moon.[14]

In the case of Shakespeare, it was an Indian Prince who guided him on his journey. Shakespeare delegated Berowne, a character in *Love's Labour's Lost*, to spell out the nature of the Guide:

> By fixing it upon a fairer eye,
> Who dazzling so, that eye shall be his heed,
> And give him light that it was blinded by.
> Study is like the heaven's glorious sun,
> That will not be deep search'd with saucy looks ...
> (*Love's Labour's Lost*, I.1)

Shakespeare states that one may hope for a successful journey only by focusing one's attention upon a guide ("By fixing it upon a fairer eye"). Only with the help of a guide is it possible to grasp the dazzling light of truth ("that eye shall be his heed"). Then, the guide will pass on hidden wisdom ("And give him light that it was blinded by"). This study is like looking at heaven's glorious sun, which cannot be penetrated by arrogant eyes ("That will not be deep-search'd with saucy looks").

---

[14] *Me and Rumi*, William C. Chittick (Fons Vitae, 2004).

## Here stand we in the Vinter's Row

The announcement of the forceful occasion is not perceptible to everyone. People respond to the arrival of Day's herald in accordance with their inner states. In the following quatrain, the "tavern" is a symbolic description of the world. The Poet is one of the tavern's patrons. He is surrounded by regulars, i.e., ordinary men and women. The regulars are not perceptive enough to recognize the arrival of the forceful occasion. They welcome this day as any other day. They are lining up and demand from the tavern keeper their usual "bowls" of routine pleasures, excitement, and short-lived desires:

2

Then shouts ring out among us at the tavern:
'Rise too, you good-for-nothing tavern lad!
Refill our empty bowls with today's measure
Before the measure of our lives be filled!'

For the regulars, life will go through its predetermined and fixed course.

## The First Counsel: Favour my bowl of crystal

The Guide is also in the tavern. The Guide is able to recognize those among the tavern's patrons who are capable of discharging correctly their duty. Those who are perceptive enough to recognize him will be invited to go on the journey.

The Guide approaches the Poet and addresses him as "my Saki." In this way he indicates that he has chosen him as his disciple:

3

'Loud crows the cock for his dawn drink, my Saki!'
'Here stand we in the Vinter's Row, my Saki!'
'Is this an hour for prayer? Silence, my Saki!'
'Defy old custom, Saki; drink your fill!'

The Poet is surprised that instead of a customary prayer, the Guide insists on starting the day with a drink.

The Guide refers to the Poet as "Rarest of lads." He tells him that this is the occasion he had been waiting for, for a long time. He may profit from it by serving him and pouring "red wine" into *his* bowl. As in the legend, the Poet may refill the Guide's bowl by correctly discharging his service:

4

> Rarest of lads, rising to greet the dawn;
> Favour my bowl of crystal, pour red wine!
> This moment filched from the grey corpse of night
> We long may sigh for, never repossess.

The Guide's bowl is made out of crystal. By asking the Poet to pour red wine into his bowl of crystal, he demonstrates allegorically the transmuting effect of wine:

> because of the wine's pureness
> and the crystal clarity of the glass
> the color of glass and wine were confused.
> All is glass – or, no, all is wine.[15]

In words of Seyyed Hossein Nasr, "The Truth, which is like a crystal or a shining star in the mind, becomes wine when it is lived and realized."[16]

The Guide compares the beginning of the journey to the arrival of a new Season. The new Season is marked by the appearance of clusters of white blossoms on trees and scents of blooming flowers. The beauty and scents of the white blossoms awake live hearts.[17] It is a time for tasting the fruits planted at the time of Moses and breathing in the air filled with Jesus' love:

---

[15] *Divine Flashes*, Fakhruddin 'Iraqi (Translated by W.C. Chittick and P.L. Wilson, Paulist Press, 1982).

[16] Preface to *Divine Flashes* (see Note #15).

[17] The term *heart* can have several meanings. It is used to indicate (i) the heart faculty, (ii) subtle layers of the heart faculty, or (iii) the inner being which includes the subtle faculties of heart and intellect. "Live heart" refers to an inner state where the heart faculty is stirred (awaken) by the presence of an evolutionary impulse (symbolically indicated by the beauty and scents of the white blossom).

5

Now that our world finds riches within reach,
Live hearts awake and hanker for wide plains
Where every bough is blanched by Moses-hand
And every breeze perfumed by Jesus-breath.

The reference to Moses and Jesus complies with the sequence of evolutionary impulses that were made available to man. For the purpose of a symbolic illustration of their effects, they may be described as a spectrum of evolutionary energies which were released on the Earth at different times in its planetary history. Each mode of energy was needed for a specific stage of the evolutionary process; each mode of energy was higher in its developmental potential than the one before. These gradually increasing potentialities are symbolically alluded to in the following words written by Omar Suhrawardi, a disciple of Abdul-Qadir of Gilan:

The Seed of Divine Wisdom
was sown in the time of Adam
germed in the time of Noah
budded in the time of Abraham
became a tree in the time of Moses
gave fruits in the time of Jesus
and produced pure wine in the time of Mohammed.[18]

Therefore, *drunkenness* corresponds to the seventh *age* of the evolutionary sequence. In other words, in the Guide's presence, the travellers ("Live hearts") may taste *fruits* planted during the

---

[18] Editor's Note to *The Authentic Rubaiyyat of Omar Khayaam* (see Note #11).

previous seasons, breath-in *perfume* and drink *wine* that were previously prepared for them. Such an occasion has often been compared by poets to the nightingale falling in love with a rose in a garden. The nightingale is prescribing *wine* to the travellers:

6

> A glorious morning, neither hot nor dank,
> With cheeks of roses newly bathed in dew;
> The nightingale, in Pahlevi, prescribes
> For every sallower cheek: 'Wine, wine and wine!'

Ordinary wine gives a hangover:

> And the wine that comes of grape juice is not free from headache.
> (*Divan-e Shams-e Tabrizi* [19])

While the drink offered by the nightingale produces an awakened inner state which allows one to realize that:

> Before there was garden and vine and grape in this world,
> Our soul was intoxicated with immortal wine.
> (*Divan-e Shams-e Tabrizi* [20])

---

[19] See Note #7.
[20] Ibid.

## Why should I blush

Now we hear the Poet. He refers to two kinds of wine. He compares daily pleasures and desires to ordinary wine. He realizes that these ordinary indulgences have kept him away from true wine. He discovers that now is "rose-time," the right time to experience true drunkenness:

7

>Most guiltily each morning I determine
>From wine in bowl or goblet to abstain;
>But this is rose-time - Lord, why should I blush
>So soon of my repentance to repent?

Yet, the Poet is somehow hesitant to commit himself to *drunkenness*. It is this moment of hesitation that prompts the Guide to deliver his second counsel.

## The Second Counsel: Laugh at long-term credit

The Guide explains that ordinary life, like ordinary intoxication, is a form of illusion. He gives as example the appearances and disappearances of great cultures and cities of the past, such as Balkh and Bagdad. Our physical existence is time-limited. It does not matter whether we perceive our experiences as pleasant or bitter. Our exit from the physical world will have no effect on it. After our departure, the Moon will continue her predetermined course:

8

> Life passes. What is Balkh? What is Baghdad?
> The cup fills - should we care whether with bitter
> Or sweet? Drink on! Know that long after us
> The Moon must keep her long-determined course.

The Guide uses the image of the rose to draw a parallel to man's life. The rose is as temporary as life itself. Like all earthly things, the rose's petals turn into dust:

## 9

Rest in the rose's shade, though winds have burst
A world of blossom; petals fall to dust -
Jamsheds and Khusros by the hundred thousand
Lie tumbled by a similar stroke of time.

This fate is common to all, whether ordinary men or famous kings like Jamshed and military commanders like Khurso. Therefore, there is no value in offering thanks to Hatim Tai for his remarkable generosity or in admiring ancient kings like Kawus, Kobad or heroes like Rustum. But a sip of *wine* may outdo the victories and glories of those famous men and cultures of the past:

## 10

One ample draught outdoes the fame of Kawus,
Kobad the Glorious or Imperial Tus.
Friend, never bow your neck even to Rustum
Nor proffer thanks even to Hatim Tai.

The Guide invites the Poet to join him in a meditation. By forging a bond with his Guide, the Poet may be exposed to wide plains "Where every bough is blanched by Moses-hand/And every breeze perfumed by Jesus-breath." The Guide refers to himself and his disciple as "us two alone", *me* and *you*. In this way the Guide indicates that there is still a separation between him and the Poet. In this context, *you* refers to the Poet's unrefined ego, his ordinary and still dominating self faculty. This separation will remain in place as long as the Poet's attention is focused on him-self.

While on the "wide plains," one mancel loaf, a haunch of mutton and a gourd of wine are enough to experience a joy that is beyond a "Sultan's bounty":


11

Should our day's portion be one mancel loaf,
A haunch of mutton and a gourd of wine
Set for us two alone on the wide plain,
No Sultan's bounty could evoke such joy.


While being together with his Guide, the haunch of mutton is substituted by a sheaf of poems. In other words, the Poet's attention is gradually shifted from the physical world onto spiritual nourishment. In this way, the quality of the bond between the Guide and the Poet is gradually brought onto a higher level:


12

A gourd of red wine and a sheaf of poems -
A bare subsistence, half a loaf, not more -
Supplied us two alone in the free desert:
What Sultan could we envy on his throne?


The Guide tells the Poet that there is no substitute for *wine*. All promises about future rewards, such as Heaven and luscious houris, are a trap for greedy people. It is a waste of time to think about future credits and other promises. Now is the time to cash-in:

### 13

> They say that Eden is bejewelled with houris;
> I answer that grape-nectar has no price -
> So laugh at long-term credit, stick to coin,
> Though distant drums beguile your greedy ear.

The Guide advises the Poet to "stick to coin." He continues his counsel by using the rose allegory. He compares rose petals to coins:

### 14

> The Rose cried: 'I am generous of largesse
> And laughter. Laughingly my petals blow
> Across the world; the ribbons of my purse
> Snap and its load of coin flies everywhere.'

The use of the "Rose" in this quatrain may be explained with the help of Rumi's and Shakespeare's writings. The following story by Rumi helps to grasp the meaning of the laughing rose:

A certain lover recounted to his mistress all the services he had done, and all the toils he had undergone for her sake. He said, "For your sake I did such and such, in this war I suffered wounds from arrows and spears. My wealth, strength and fame are gone. On account of my love for you many a misfortune has befallen me. No dawn found me asleep or laughing; no evening found me with money or means to live." What he had tasted of bitterness and sorrow he was recounting to her in detail, point by point. Not for the sake of reproach. No. He was displaying a hundred testimonies of the trueness of his love. For men of reason a single indication is enough, but how should the longing of lovers be removed thereby? The lover repeats his tale unworriedly: how should a fish be satisfied with a mere indication so as to refrain from the limpid water? There was a fire in him. He did not know what it was, but on account of its heat he was weeping like a candle. The beloved said, "You have done all this; yet open your ear wide and apprehend well. For you have not done what is the root of the root of love and duty. What you have done is only the branches." The lover said to her, "Tell me, what is that root?" She said, "The root thereof is to die and become nothing. You have done all else, but you have not died, you are still living. You have to die if you are a self-sacrificing friend!" The lover accordingly gave up his life: like the rose, he played away his head, laughing and rejoicing.

(*Mathnawi*, Book *V*)

The laughing rose represents the moment of dying to our worldly attachments. The allegorical meaning of the transformation of petals into coins is explained by Shakespeare in *Sonnet 54*:

Oh how much more doth beauty beauteous seem
By that sweet ornament which truth doth give!
The rose looks fair, but fairer we it deem
For that sweet odour, which doth in it live.
The canker-blooms have full as deep a dye
As the perfumed tincture of the roses,
Hang on such thorns, and play as wantonly,
When summer's breath their masked buds discloses;
But for their virtue only is their show,
They live unwoo'd, and unrespected fade,

> Die to themselves. Sweet roses do not so,
> Of their sweet deaths, are sweetest odours made:
>> And so of you, beauteous and lovely youth,
>> When that shall vade, by verse distills your truth.
> (*Sonnet 54*)

In this Sonnet Shakespeare explains that a rose's beauty may be
preserved through the process of distillation ("The rose looks fair,
but fairer we it deem/For that sweet odour, which doth in it live").
He compares the domestic rose with its wild cousins. The
wildflowers' only virtue is their outward look. They do not have
such a sweet fragrance as the rose; only their external appearance is
similar ("Hang on such thorns, and play as wantonly,/When
summer's breath their masked buds discloses"). The wildflowers
are sterile; they grow idly and fade away unnoticed ("But for their
virtue only is their show,/They live unwoo'd, and unrespected
fade"). Left to themselves, they die alone leaving no traces ("die to
themselves"). But when the rose dies, its *essence* is transmuted into
the sweetest fragrance ("Sweet roses do not so,/Of their sweet
deaths, are sweetest odours made"). In this way, Shakespeare
indicates that man's inner being may be distilled and preserved
("And so of you, beauteous and lovely youth,/When that shall
vade, by verse distills your truth"). In other words, "coins" are the
rose's fragrance; the poet's largesse is his poems.

In the following quatrain, the Guide warns the Poet that if he
remains attached to the wine of the "regulars," he will end up just
like the canker. He sarcastically implies that the Poet should get a
drink ("Command our tavern-lad to fetch you drink"); by doing so,
the Poet would prove that he is just a fool ("Fool, your dry corpse
will be no treasure trove/For proud posterity to disinter"):

## 15

Before Fate springs her ambush for your life,
Command our tavern-lad to fetch you drink.
Fool, your dry corpse will be no treasure trove
For proud posterity to disinter!

In the world that has been modelled to please our sensual desires
(the wine of the "regulars"), we are just like "a snowdrift on the
sand." We last for no longer than "two days or three, then thawed
and gone":

## 16

Think of this world as modelled at your whim,
Perfectly trimmed for you from east to west;
Yet know yourself a snowdrift on the sand
Heaped for two days or three, then thawed and gone.

Our experiences are given to us in accordance with our ability to
use them. We accumulate and store them. They become available
when, later on, certain happenings require them. First, however,
one has to arrive at the state of "being nothing" before an
experience may be used in a constructive manner. So, the Guide
advises the Poet that he may think of this world as a ruined
caravanserai or as a stable of day-with-night. All former and
famous kings spent time in this "Stable." Now, they all are gone:

## 17

This ruined caravanserai, called Earth -
Stable of Day-with-Night, a piebald steed;
Former pavilion of a hundred Jamsheds;
A hundred Bahrams' one-time hall of state;

All the most powerful kings and hunters, like Bahram who was known for his fondness for hunting wild-ass ("onagers"), ended-up in their graves:

## 18

A Palace gorged in by gigantic Bahram -
The vixen whelps there and the lion nods.
Bahram, who hunted none but onagers,
Lies tumbled in a pitfall called the grave.

A similar line of thought about the transience of kings is delivered by Hamlet in his exchange with King Claudius. Hamlet describes how a king might end up in the bowels of a beggar (*Hamlet*, IV.3):

Hamlet:
   A man may fish with the worm that hath eat of a king, and eat of the fish that hath fed of that worm.

Claudius:
   What dost you mean by this?

Hamlet:
   Nothing but to show you how a king may go a progress through the guts of a beggar.

In other words, material things may be turned into other forms for they are all built from the same ingredients. Yet, man's immaterial soul (inner being) has the potential to be transmuted into higher forms, as Arif Shah stated so directly:

> Man and the earth are made of the same things. Everything that is in us can be found in the earth. Water and salt and minerals and elements, all mixed up and held together by this thing which is called the mind. It's all governed by the heart.[21]

The above remark helps to grasp the meaning of Falstaff's "little kingdom" where the heart is the captain. Through the development of this inner kingdom, it is possible to free oneself from that earthly cycle and rise up to a higher form of living. The Guide refers allegorically to this higher form as the scent of flowers that emerge from black earth:

19

> Each rose or tulip bed that you encounter
> Is sure to mark a king's last resting-place,
> While scented violets, rising from black soil,
> Record the burial of some lovely girl.

Laertes in *Hamlet* also expresses hope that, after her death, his beautiful sister Ophelia will rise up as scented violets. In this way, Shakespeare indicates Ophelia's symbolic function:

---

[21] *The Mines of Light*, Arif Shah (Pick and Shovel, Los Angeles. 2016).

> Lay her i' the earth,
> And from her fair and unpolluted flesh
> May violets spring!
> (*Hamlet*, *V.1*)

The Guide tells the Poet that he may be able to find out that his inner being can see everything that ever existed, or ever will exist; it can see further and more completely than he could ever even imagine. He describes such a spiritual state as being capable of seeing the evidence of a beauty of angelic kind in green cresses and flowers:

### 20

> Green cresses, also, masking a stream's bank
> Start up from creatures of angelic kind.
> Tread softly on such evidence of beauty:
> Red lips and rosy cheeks fast slumbering.

Beauty of "angelic kind" is a symbolic reference to *beauty* that may be perceived through the subtle faculties. The activation of the subtle faculties of intellect and heart revivifies man and transforms him into a Perfect Man:

> Man, would never develop any further physically. The body, having reached its apogee, would destroy the mind, unless the heart were made alert to its responsibilities, reformed, regenerated and in turn revivified the body. Then the mind and the body would constitute one organ, and this is what the Perfect Man actually means.[22]

---

[22] *Among the Dervishes*, O. M. Burke (Octagon Press, 1973).

The Guide concludes this counsel by saying that the Poet should not worry about tomorrow's sorrow. He has a chance to experience "this paradisal Now":

21

> Never anticipate tomorrow's sorrow.
> Live always in this paradisal Now -
> Fated however soon to house, instead,
> With others gone these seven thousand years.

"These seven thousand years" is a reference to the symbolic seven *ages* of the evolutionary sequence (see the quatrain #5). These are the seven spiritual millennia during which the entire spectrum of evolutionary energies was made available to man. As a result, ordinary man has been provided with the potential of arriving at the state of the Perfect Man and experiencing "this paradisal Now."

The Guide encourages the Poet to live in the present and not count on tomorrow's successes. If he is preoccupied with tomorrow, he will not be able to fulfil his potential and will fatedly but worthlessly only serve as food for worms.

# My tavern comrades

Now we hear the Poet again. The Poet sadly notices that his comrades vanish one by one from the tavern:

22

My tavern comrades vanish one by one,
Innocent victims of Death's furtive stroke.
All had been honest drinkers, but all failed,
Two rounds before the last, to drain their bowls.

The Poet's comrades were honest drinkers but they all failed to sustain their spiritual intoxication. During their lives, they did not manage to pass beyond the stage of *drunkenness* and experience the next stages of the process ("Two rounds before the last").

Spiritual *drunkenness* is an intermediate step, which has to be fully experienced first before the next step can be taken. In other words, spiritual *ecstasy* is not the objective of spiritual undertaking. At first, *drunkenness* is forbidden. Then, *drunkenness* is required. At a specific time, *drunkenness* has to be abandoned:

Do not sit intoxicated at the door: come into the house quickly.
(*Divan-e Shams-e Tabrizi*[23])

---

[23] See Note #7.

Therefore, there is a time when *drinking* is needed; and there is a time when such *drinking* may impede one's progress. Mark Antony in Shakespeare's *Antony and Cleopatra* is one such honest drinker who is too much attached to his *drunkenness*. When Octavius Caesar interrupts the wine drinking festivities to remind him that there is more serious business to be done, Mark Antony's answer is the most telling phrase describing his inner state:

> Be a child o'th' time.
>
> (*Antony and Cleopatra, II.7*)

Mark Antony tries to persuade Octavius Caesar to forget duty and urges him to drink until they reach complete lethargy:

> Come, let's all take hands,
> Till that the conquering wine hath steep'd our sense
> In soft and delicate Lethe.
> (*Antony and Cleopatra, II.7*)

In this particular context, "Lethe" (lethargy) indicates spiritual intoxication. The main purpose of the availability of such states is not their enjoyment but gaining capacity for carrying on additional responsibilities. However, Mark Antony prefers to enjoy the moment. He neglects his duties and chooses to enjoy his drunkenness. His tendency to live according to the moment, with little regard for the overall process, is one of the factors of his failure.

Now it is time for the Guide to explain what these "Two rounds before the last" are. In the following counsel, he outlines the coming stages of the Poet's journey.

## The Third Counsel: Study your essence

The Guide tells the Poet that his journey consists of four distinctive stages, i.e., rising-up, experiencing gratitude and joy, being freed from womb and tomb, and truly living and loving:

23

Rise up, why mourn this transient world of men?
Pass your whole life in gratitude and joy.
Had humankind been freed from womb and tomb,
When would your turn have come to live and love?

The first stage is the initiation (rising-up), i.e., the commencement of the spiritual journey. At this point, the ordinary faculties, or *raw* materials, are getting ready to be *cooked* by coming experiences. This stage of the journey was announced in the first quatrain. At this stage the disciple learns about the limitations of ordinary mind ("this transient world"); he discovers that he is a prisoner of the physical world. He is expected to abandon ("mourn") ordinary thinking patterns that are driven by intellectual and emotional reflexes.

At the second stage, the disciple is required to submerge himself in the presence of his Guide. It is then that he experiences *drunkenness*, i.e., the first taste of "gratitude and joy." As indicated in the previous quatrain, it was at this stage that Khayaam's comrades abandoned the journey.

The third stage corresponds to the disciple's experience of "being freed from womb and tomb," when he *dies* to his earthly existence. It is in this context that Prince Hall in Shakespeare's *Henry IV* reminds Falstaff that he owes his death to God:

> Why, thou owest God a death.
> (*Henry IV, Part 1, V.1*)

The fourth stage refers to the disciple's spiritual *rebirth*, i.e., when the disciple experiences fuller *life* and *love* ("to live and love"). He escapes from the prison of dimensions and goes beyond these dimensions.

This means that, at this point of his journey, the Poet is going through the experiences of the second stage of the process. He experiences the first manifestations of true gratitude and joy. These experiences are symbolically described as "love-songs" and "kisses":

## 24

> Allow no shadow of regret to cloud you,
> No absurd grief to overcast your days.
> Never renounce love-songs, or lawns, or kisses
> Until your clay lies mixed with elder clay.

The Poet's inner being is gradually permeated with his Guide's essence. The Guide describes this particular phase of the process as the mixing of "your clay" with "elder clay."

In practice, such permeation leads gradually to the realization that neither intellectual discourses nor emotional attachments to various doctrines and beliefs are capable of providing satisfying answers. Technically, this means that the mind is still working through two separate sides of the brain. However, while at this stage, one may experience brief manifestations of the subtle layers of the intellect, i.e., when both sides of the brain start to work together in harmony. This higher function of the mind is manifested by the appearance of an *inner voice* or an *inner guide*. The following quatrain refers to this inner guide who, at such brief moments, may fleetingly leap "out of hiding":

## 25

Some ponder long on doctrine and belief,
Some teeter between certitude and doubt.
Suddenly out of hiding leaps the Guide
With: 'Fools, the Way is neither that nor this.'

The Guide emphasizes that intellectual debates and discussions are useless; they are just various forms of manifestations of raw ego. What is needed instead is total *drunkenness*, i.e., immersing oneself in the Guide's essence:

## 26

Most of them, gone before we go, my Saki,
Drowse in their dusty bed of pride, my Saki.
Drink yet again and hear the truth at last:
'Whatever words they spoke were wind, my Saki.'

The Guide advises the Poet to make sure that he drinks enough, so he may experience complete *drunkenness* before he dies. Just like Barnardine in Shakespeare's *Measure for Measure* who needs more time to "prepare me," therefore he refuses to be executed because he is not ready yet:

> Friar, not I; I have been drinking hard all night, and I will have more time to prepare me, or they shall beat out my brains with billets. I will not consent to die this day, that's certain.
> (*Measure for Measure, IV.3*)

The Guide continues his explanation by saying that all cafe philosophers are gone, snoozing senselessly in their dusty graves, "Whatever words they spoke were wind." Therefore, "Study your essence" like those "most perfect of our kind" who were able to mount "the soaring Burak of their thoughts" and experience higher worlds:

27

> Yet those who proved most perfect of our kind
> Mounted the soaring Burak of their thoughts.
> Study your essence: like the Firmament,
> Your head will turn and turn, vertiginously.

Such moments of inner inspiration (*mounting the Burak of one's thoughts*) may be induced by momentarily emptying one's mind of shallow thoughts. This may be compared to clearing one's mind from mechanical thinking by a centrifugal force that is symbolically represented, for example, by a whirling dance. In such moments, one may get in contact with one's inner voice.

The Guide continues his counsel by emphasizing that the spiritual teaching does not have anything to do with conventional training methods:

28

> In childhood once we crouched before our teacher,
> Growing content, in time, with what he taught;
> How does the story end? What happened to us?
> We came like water and like wind were gone.

Formal trainings do not affect man's inner being because they are focused on physical senses and ordinary faculties. These senses and faculties are incapable of handling questions such as why in the world we came, or went, or were. At best, we may only conclude that we came down, like rain from somewhere above ("We came like water"); and we will be gone somewhere, like mist and clouds pulled by wind ("and like wind were gone").

## No sage stood there to greet me

Now the Poet describes how he has come to his understanding that searching for knowledge on his own was in vain. He realized that, even at the summits of his poetical inspiration, he was incapable of solving the mystery of life. This is why he decided to look for a guide:

29

When falcon-like I darted from my world
Of mystery, upward and upward flying,
No sage stood there to greet me with the truth;
So back I dived by the same narrow door.

Trying to solve the mystery of life on one's own does not bring meaningful results. The Poet's conclusion coincides with Rumi's advice:

Do not, then, travel alone on a Way that you have not seen at all, do not turn your head away from the Guide.
(*Mathnawi*, Book I)

In the next quatrain, the Guide emphasizes the limitations of the Poet's intellect.

## The Fourth Counsel: Intellect proves nugatory

The Guide says that it does not matter how hard we employ our intellect to try to learn or teach, "All intellect be sure, proves nugatory":

30

Man's brain has never solved the eternal Why
Nor foraged past the frontier set for thought.
All intellect be sure, proves nugatory,
However hard we either teach or learn.

Rumi's famous statement contains a similar message:

The intellect is but a muzzle for spiritual insight, but among all creatures it is only man whose inner heart contains a precious jewel.
(*Mathnawi, Book I*)

The meaning of "precious jewel" is further elaborated by the Duke Senior in Shakespeare's *As You Like It*:

Sweet are the uses of adversity
Which like the toad, ugly and venomous,
Wears yet a precious jewel in his head;
(*As You Like It, II.1*)

It is this precious jewel hidden in the mind that constitutes man's evolutionary potential. But only those who are capable to overcome their nugatory intellectuality may find this treasure, i.e., develop an organ of supracognitive perception.

## I have unveiled all astral mysteries

The Poet reflects on the Guide's last counsel. He observes that his intellect has been incapable of answering in a satisfactory manner his questions about his origin, life and destiny:

### 31

In agitation I was brought to birth
And learned nothing from life but wonder at it;
Reluctantly we leave, still uninformed
Why in the world we came, or went, or were.

So, he decided to "wrap a cloth about your loins" and start a journey in order to escape from the misery of the ordinary world:

### 32

My presence here has been no choice of mine;
Fate hounds me most unwillingly away.
Rise, wrap a cloth about your loins, my Saki,
And swill away the misery of this world.

He continues his meditation on the limitation of his choices of coming, becoming and being in this world:

## 33

Were the choice mine to come, should I have come?
Or to become? What might I have become?
What better fortune could I then have chanced on
Than not to come, become, or even be?

Although his knowledge of astronomy allowed him to get away from astrological deceit and fraud, this did not help him to learn more about the working of "Fate's design":

## 34

Earth's Perigee to Saturn's Apogee -
I have unveiled all astral mysteries:
Breaking the barriers of deceit and fraud,
Leaping all obstacles but Fate's design.

The Poet admits that his intellect is incapable of breaking the eternal Cypher. It is this moment of sincerity that prompts the Guide to deliver the next counsel.

## The Fifth Counsel: Cypher proves too hard to break

Right now, says the Guide, the Poet may hear some whispers, but his inner voice still remains behind a curtain. It is this curtain that makes "you" and "I," i.e., separates the Poet from true reality. As long as "I" is the main operating entity of one's being, one cannot "learn the inmost secret":

35

Not you, not I, can learn the inmost secret:
The eternal Cypher proves too hard to break.
Behind God's Curtain voices babble of us
But when it parts, where then shall we two be?

The "Curtain" is made out of previous experiences that include disappointments, short-lived excitements, fears, confusion and uncertainty. Our emotional and intellectual reflexes are merely reflections that bounce back from one's inner curtain. Only when the curtain is torn down, "you" and "I" may become *one*.

The Poet's next task on his journey is to prepare himself for this particular experience.

## My inner ear could hear

While *drinking*, the Poet partially awakens his inner perception. This experience is manifested by the appearance of his inner voice:

### 36

Greedily to the bowl my lips I pressed
And asked how might I sue for green old age.
Pressing its lips to mine it muttered darkly:
'Drink up! Once gone, you shall return no more!'

The clayish bowl is a container. Therefore, it may only speak from its own perspective, the perspective of a worldly thing. Worldly things are concerned only with time and space limited pleasures and desires:

### 37

This jug was, ages past, a doleful lover
Like me - who had pursued a dream, like me.
This handle at its neck was once an arm
Entwined about some neck he loved too well.

Preoccupations with worldly desires ("he loved too well") prevent us from fulfilling our dreams.

Rumi also described this form of manifestation of one's inner voice. He used King Solomon's conversation with plants and herbs to illustrate this kind of experience:

> When King Solomon came to the throne, he built a temple.
> Every morning he saw that a new plant had grown there. And
> he would ask, "Tell me what is your name and use. What kind
> of medicine are you? To whom you are hurtful and for whom
> are you useful?" Then each plant would tell its effect and
> name, saying "I am life to that one, and death to this one. I am
> poison to this one, and sugar to that one. This is my name that
> was inscribed on the Tablet by the pen of the Divine decree."
> (*Mathnawi, Book IV*)

King Solomon communicated with plants. The Poet hears the "sighs and groans" of batches of clay:

38

> Yesterday in the market stood a potter
> Pounding relentlessly his batch of clay.
> My inner ear could hear it sigh and groan:
> 'Brother, I once was like you. Treat me gently!'

It does not matter whether you are a clayish king or a clayish beggar. The Master is able to make a Man out of you:

## 39

> In the potter's workroom, shadowed by the wheel,
> I pondered, watching how the Master made
> Handles and covers for his jugs and pitchers
> From clay - from hands of kings, from beggars' feet.

This last quatrain is echoed in Hamlet's meditation on the fate of Alexander the Great:

> Alexander died, Alexander was buried, Alexander returneth to dust, the dust is earth, of earth we make loam; and why of that loam whereto he was converted might they not stop a beer-barrel?
> (*Hamlet*, V.1)

The clayish container, either in the form of a wine pitcher, a beer-barrel plug or a man, remains in this world. But man's inner being, however, is capable of breaking through time and space limitations. The Poet gradually discovers that by following his Guide's counsels, the content of his clayish container can be transmuted into a new Man.

## 40

> I wandered further down the Potters' Row.
> Continuously they tried new skills on clay;
> Yet some, devoid of vision, never noted
> The ancestral dust on every turning wheel.

The Poet further realizes that it is not the novelty or ingenuity of various dogmas, arts or philosophy ("new skills") that may lead to the other worlds. Shakespeare expressed a similar observation in *Sonnet 123*:

> Thy pyramids built up with newer might
> To me are nothing novel, nothing strange;
> They are but dressings of a former sight.
> (*Sonnet 123*)

It is the presence of "the ancestral dust," that is to say, the Guide's *essence* that constitutes the crucial element of the soul's transmutation.

## The Sixth Counsel: Fancy yourself no longer there

The Guide says that each moment of a disciple's true drunkenness ("Each drop of wine") may serve as medicine for "some sore heart":

41

Each drop of wine that Saki negligently
Spills on the ground may quench the fires of grief
In some sore heart. All praise to Him who offers
Such medicine to relieve its melancholy!

A medicine for sore hearts is available, but it offers only half a cure. The other half is the effort of the person itself. Only those who are capable of recognizing this sort of medicine may fully benefit from it. In *The Merchant of Venice*, Shakespeare refers to such recognition as the ability of hearing the music of the spheres ("harmony"):

Such harmony is in immortal souls,
But whilst this muddy vesture of decay
Doth grossly close it in, we cannot hear it.
(*The Merchant of Venice, V.1*)

In other words, those whose souls are still maculated by worldly desires ("this muddy vesture of decay") cannot respond correctly to this medicine. Shakespeare used the character of Antonio to illustrate how one's inability to recognize the presence of such "harmony" may cause sadness, worries, and melancholy:

In sooth, I know not why I am so sad;
It wearies me; you say it wearies you;
But how I caught it, found it, or came by it,
What stuff 'tis made of, whereof it is born,
I am to learn;
And such a want-wit sadness makes of me,
That I have much ado to know myself.
(*The Merchant of Venice, I.1*)

Antonio cannot be merry and he does not know the reason of his melancholy. He realizes, however, that he would have to know himself much better in order to figure it out ("I have much ado to know myself"). In this way, Shakespeare informs us that Antonio's soul is still grossly closed by "this muddy vesture of decay."

The Guide explains that *wine* may pass through "this muddy vesture of decay" and reach the Poet's inner heart. This is the only way to free oneself before "brutal Time will strike you down":

42

Raise the bowl high, like tulip-cups at Nauroz,
And if the moon-faced one has time to spare
Drink gloriously deep, for brutal Time
Will strike you down with never a warning yell.

The Poet's ability to hear his inner voice is like the arrival of spiritual spring ("Nowruz" marks the first day of spring and the beginning of the year in the Persian calendar). The Guide reaffirms that he provided the Poet with *medicine*. Now it is up to the Poet himself to use it correctly:

## 43

Avoid all greed and envy, unperturbed
By permutations, foul succeeding fair;
Possess your bowl, play with your loved one's curls;
Soon the whole scene must vanish past recourse.

The Poet has to avoid all greed, envy and be unperturbed by life experiences when successes are followed by failures. For the time being, he has to be dedicated to the discipline of the path ("Possess your bowl") and enjoy that what the path offers ("play with your loved one's curls").

In the following quatrain, for the first time the Guide addresses the Poet as Khayaam. At the same time, the Guide emphasizes that Khayaam is capable of getting "drunk with love" and he should "Fancy yourself no longer there." This means that the Poet is being prepared for the third stage of his journey when he is going to be "freed from womb and tomb." Now, he should enjoy being "bedded with your heart's delight." No longer should he fear departing from this world:

## 44

Khayaam, should you be drunk with love, rejoice!
Or bedded with your heart's delight, rejoice!
Your end is no more than the whole world's end.
Fancy yourself no longer there; then smile.

In other words, the Guide prepares Khayaam for the experience of *to die before dying*. Here is an observation by Rumi that refers to this particular experience:

> How should anyone not die to self, unless he be a vile wretch?
> (*Mathnawi, Book I*)

Similarly, several Shakespearean characters alluded to this particular stage of the spiritual journey:

Othello(*V.2*):
> For, in my sense, 'tis happiness to die.

Friar Francis in *Much Ado About Nothing (IV.1)*:
> Come, lady, die to live;

Friar Lawrence in *Romeo and Juliet (IV.5)*:
> She's not well married that lives married long;
> But she's best married that dies married young.

Viola in *Twelfth Night (V.1)*:
> And I, most jocund, apt and willingly,
> To do you rest, a thousand deaths would die.

The Guide advises Khayaam that he should not pay too much attention to his past and future. Such thoughts and preoccupations would diminish his inner potential. His separation from his essence is the cause of his discontent and bitterness. Therefore, "Drink, never cast your essence to the winds":

45

> Oppose all resurrections of your past,
> Resent no anguish still prepared for you,
> Dwell lightly on your entrance and your exit -
> Drink, never cast your essence to the winds.

If you stop drinking, says the Guide, you will end-up like all those who never entered onto the path. Jaques in Shakespeare's *As You Like It* refers to such *non-drinkers* as "merely players" whose life consists of seven ordinary *ages*:

> All the world's a stage,
> And all the men and women merely players;
> They have their exits and their entrances,
> And one man in his time plays many parts,
> His acts being seven ages. At first the infant,
> Mewling and puking in the nurse's arms.
> And then the whining schoolboy, with his satchel
> And shining morning face, creeping like snail
> Unwillingly to school. And then the lover,
> Sighing like furnace, with a woeful ballad
> Made to his mistress' eyebrow. Then a soldier,
> Full of strange oaths, and bearded like the pard,
> Jealous in honour, sudden and quick in quarrel,
> Seeking the bubble reputation
> Even in the cannon's mouth. And then the justice,
> In fair round belly with good capon lin'd,
> With eyes severe and beard of formal cut,
> Full of wise saws and modern instances;
> And so he plays his part. The sixth age shifts
> Into the lean and slipper'd pantaloon,
> With spectacles on nose, and pouch on side,
> His youthful hose, well sav'd, a world too wide
> For his shrunk shank, and his big manly voice,
> Turning again toward childish treble, pipes
> And whistles in his sound. Last scene of all,
> That ends this strange eventful history,
> Is second childishness, and mere oblivion,

Sans teeth, sans eyes, sans taste, sans every thing.
(*As You Like It, II.7*)

Jaques' description of the seven "ages" applies to the life of an ordinary man. Such a man is ignorant of the possibility of a fuller life. Instead of becoming a Perfect Man, such a man ends up his life in "mere oblivion," without teeth, without eyes, without taste, without everything.

The Guide, therefore, advises Khayaam "Dwell lightly on your entrance and your exist." And when his turn comes to *die*, he should refrain from tears, be merry, and "Lift high the bowl, then drain it to its lees":

46

This vast, unmeasured, universal vault
Offers one bowl for all mankind to drink.
When your turn comes, refrain from tears, be merry,
Lift high the bowl, then drain it to its lees!

The Guide's advice is identical to that offered by Sanai:

and not until
You've twice drunk wine and headache to the lees,
Will I say of you, 'There goes a man!'[24]

The Guide adds that when Khayaam experiences *death*, he will be ashamed of himself for having been attached to his bodily limitations for so long:

---

[24] *The Walled Garden of Truth*, Hakim Sanai (Octagon Press, 1974).

### 47

Dear love, when you are free to slough your skin
And become naked spirit, soaring far
Across God's Empyrean, you will blush
That you lay cramped so long in body's gaol.


Claudio receives a similar advice from the Duke of Vienna in Shakespeare's *Measure for Measure*:

Be absolute for death: either death or life
Shall thereby be the sweeter. Reason thus with life:
If I do lose thee, I do lose a thing
That none but fools would keep. A breath thou art,
Servile to all the skyey influences,
That dost this habitation where thou keep'st
Hourly afflict. Merely, thou art death's fool,
For him thou labour'st by thy flight to shun,
And yet runn'st toward him still.
(*Measure for Measure*, III.1)


No one but a fool, says the Duke, wants to be kept in a body that is entirely controlled by planetary influences. One is just death's fool; one tries to escape away from it, but all that one is doing is running toward it.

In the next quatrain, the Guide further explains that Khayaam's physical body is like a tent; his soul is like a Sultan. Now he is required to abandon the tent. This action is encoded in Khayaam's name: *Khayaam* means *Tentmaker*. It may be decoded by the *abjad* system as *Al Ghaqi* or *Squanderer of goods*.[25] This indicates a person who does not care for the ordinary things of this world, i.e., a person who abandons his *tent*.

A squanderer of goods is one who gives away or ignores worldly goods which burden him in his voyage along the path. Such burden causes a dissipation of attention and prevents one from developing perception of other dimensions:

48

> Khayaam, your mortal carcass is a tent;
> Your soul, a Sultan; and your camp, all Time.
> The groom called Fate maps out tomorrow's march
> And strikes the tent when, Sultan-like, you move.

In order to enter the heavenly pavilion, one needs a Guide. The Guide here is that "deathless Saki" who has already drunk the Drink of the Immortals. Despite the protected entrance, the Guide is able to bring to this royal pavilion thousands of his disciples. But he may bring with him only Squanderers of goods, i.e., those who are capable of abandoning their *tents*.

---

[25] Similarly, by using the abjad system (see Note #13), the name of *Rumi* may be decoded as *Light*.

## 49

Khayaam, though this blue-stained royal pavilion,
Tautens its golden guy-ropes against entry,
A deathless Saki draws Khayaams in thousands
Like wine-bubbles out of Creation's bowl.

By abandoning their tents, the successful travelers *die* to this world.
Of course, their departure from this world does not make the
slightest dent on it. This world did not need you before your
arrival. Why would it care about your departure?

## 50

This world must long survive our poor departure,
Persisting without name or note of us.
Before we came, it never grudged our absence;
When we have gone, how can it feel regret?

The caravan of ordinary life is passing like the night. Therefore do
not waste your precious time. Do not worry about others and their
future. Immerse yourself in your Guide's *essence*:

## 51

The caravan of life passes in strangeness.
Come, seize one moment passing joyfully.
Why mourn for friends and their tomorrow, Saki?
Pour out more wine: the night is passing too.

Use wisely the time that you have got. When you are with your Guide, do not waste time on useless worries; forget about your worldly preoccupations. Instead, enjoy each moment of his *presence*:

## 52

Dear lad, steeped as you are in Mysteries,
Why should you load your heart with nameless cares?
Let projects fade away; disport yourself
In the brief hour when life detains you here.

Be aware of and cherish your breathing. The quality of your breathing is a mark of your progress:

## 53

One breath parts infidelity from faith;
Another breath parts certitude from doubt.
Yet cherish breath, never make light of it -
Is not such breath the harvest of our being?

Breath is a conduit of the divine essence; a single breath may bring you into the *Presence*.

It is said that man was made out of potter's clay and then life was breathed into him. Sometimes, breath is compared to a luminous substance, a ray of light. This is why it may be said that there are lights which ascend and lights which descend. The ascending lights are the lights of the inner being; the descending lights are those of the Eternal One. In other words, a developed man breathes in *lights* of the Eternal One; and he breathes out *lights* of his inner heart:

> When, through just desire,
> you form an image in your heart,
> breathe life into it with the breath
> -like a mighty trumpet blast-
> of those initiated in the mysteries.[26]

One of the functions of correct breathing is to nourish the farthest recesses of our deep consciousness. Through correct breathing, one provides a catalyst for the activation of the subtle faculties; it enriches them. Ordinary men breathe to sustain their level of existence; a disciple breathes to make a breakthrough into higher levels of being; a developed man breathes to maintain the breakthrough that he has made into a superior realm of being; the Guide of the Age breathes to sustain the world. It may take months or even years before a person is able to take his first real breath. It is then that he may advance his progress along the path.

---

[26] *The Abode of Spring*, Jami (included in *Four Sufi Classics*, Octagon Press, 1980).

# I breathed the letter A

Khayaam follows the previous counsel on breathing. He experiences a breakthrough when he takes in his first real breath:

54

My heart complained: 'I long for inspiration,
I long for wisdom, to be taught and learn.'
I breathed the letter A. My heart replied:
'A is enough to occupy this house.'

By experiencing the First, one can know the Last and understand All. It is in this sense that "A is enough to occupy this house" refers to the nature of true reality. This is why it is said that "The first letter of the first word of a single children's story could suffice to instruct man."[27]

Shakespeare encoded the concept of the First and the Last, Alpha and Omega, in the term MOAI. Maria in *Twelfth Night* uses the term MOAI to spell out what the supreme priority of Lady Olivia is. Shakespeare provides a couple of hints that allow decoding of this seemingly baffling term:

---

27 *Dermis Probe*, Idries Shah (Octagon Press, London 1970).

The numbers altered!

and

there is no consonancy in the sequel
(*Twelfth Night*, II.5)

There are only two (Roman) numbers there, i.e., M and I.[28] By following Shakespeare's hints, i.e., removing these two numbers and then reversing the sequel of the remaining two letters, one may find out who "doth sway" Olivia's life: *A* and *O*, i.e., *Alpha* and *Omega*, the *First* and the *Last*, a symbolic representation of the supreme priority. It is this supreme priority that guides Olivia's actions.

---

[28] At the literal level, "numbers" refer to "meter", a unit of rhythm in poetry.

## The Seventh Counsel: Destroy the form

The Guide continues to direct Khayaam through this very difficult stage of his journey. He reminds him that he will not progress as long as he pays too much attention to worldly forms. The external or worldly forms are like the changes of the Moon. The Moon may seem to move like an animal and grow like a vegetable. Both of these forms are being continuously destroyed and then renewed. But what survives is just the Moon's form. In this way, the Moon teaches us about the nothingness of form:

55

The Moon, by her own nature skilled in change,
Varies from animal form to vegetable.
Destroy the form, you destroy nothingness -
For what she seems survives her not-yet-being.

Shakespeare's King Richard II also arrives at a similar conclusion:

But whate'er I be,
Nor I, nor any man that but man is,
With nothing shall be pleas'd, till he be eas'd
With being nothing.
(*Richard II*, V.5)

One has to realize, and then accept, that he is *nothing* before he can make progress.

# I know nothing

Khayaam asks for more wine to deal with his still strong and disturbing "fires of youth." He realizes that only *wine* may quench the fever of his heart:

### 56

> Bring wine to allay the fever of my heart;
> Existence here runs as quicksilver runs.
> Rise up, for wakefulness is what sleep treasures
> And fires of youth like water drain away.

A similar attitude is expressed by the Duke of Vienna when he is seeking the assistance of Friar Thomas in Shakespeare's *Measure for Measure*. In the following observation, the Duke indicates that his purpose for pursuing Isabella is much deeper than "the dribbling dart of love":

> No; holy father, throw away that thought;
> Believe not that the dribbling dart of love
> Can pierce a complete bosom. Why I desire thee
> To give me secret harbour, hath a purpose
> More grave and wrinkled than the aims and ends
> Of burning youth.
> (*Measure for Measure, I.3*)

The Duke indicates that he is somewhat a complete man ("a complete bosom"). His purpose is more serious than "the aims and ends of burning youth."

The Poet's fleeting encounters with his inner voice have made him confused:

### 57

> Hidden you live, inscrutable as ever -
> A person sometimes, but sometimes a place,
> Showing this costly spectacle to no one -
> You, the sole audience and the actor too.

At this stage of the journey, Khayaam is simultaneously driven by his heart's desire and by his attachments to worldly attractions. He asks himself how he may know what is going to happen to him after his death when he does not even know himself:

### 58

> Could my heart know, in life, life's hidden secrets,
> Death could inform me of God's hidden secrets.
> Since I know nothing of myself today,
> What can I know tomorrow, after death?

Khayaam is still hesitant to commit himself fully to the discipline of the path. As long as he is hesitant in his actions, he will simply serve only as food for worms.

## The Eight Counsel: Choose your vintage well

In this counsel, the Guide answers the Poet's question from the previous quatrain. Once again, the Guide emphasizes that Khayaam cannot learn much about himself through logic and reason. This sort of knowledge cannot be learnt through intellectual debate:

59

Those dupes of intellect and logic die
In arguments on being or not being;
Go, ignoramus, choose your vintage well -
From dust like theirs grow none but unripe grapes.

Instead, Khayaam should focus his attention on the Guide's presence ("choose your vintage well"). Only in this way may he free himself from egocentric judgment and develop his inner being.

A spiritually developed man's inner faculties are clear and unclouded. At this stage he can see new colours, he can smell new fragrances, and he can hear the music of the spheres. Such a man acquires back-and-forth chronological versatility. He can see past and future, which means that he can verify doctrine in a way impossible to others. Going back into the past reveals the real situation. Going into the future shows how sterile or fruitful the results of an action would be. A developed man doesn't attempt to do what he knows cannot be done; all others depend on trial-and-error. In other words, reason is incapable of resolving the arguments "on being or not being." The result of *reasoning* is no more than sour grapes.

Shakespeare's Hamlet is an example of one of those "dupes of intellect and logic" who struggles with the question of "being or not being":

> To be, or not to be, that is the question:
> Whether 'tis nobler in the mind to suffer
> The slings and arrows of outrageous fortune,
> Or to take arms against a sea of troubles
> And by opposing end them.
> (*Hamlet, III.1*)

The stage "not to be" is developmentally sterile. It corresponds to ordinary life with all its suffering of "slings and arrows of outrageous fortune," just like that of the lover in Rumi's story quoted in the commentary on the quatrain #14 ("I suffered wounds from arrows and spears"). On the other hand, the stage "to be" corresponds to a spiritually developed man. This approach requires extraordinary personal effort. The soliloquy refers to such an effort as "to take arms against a sea of troubles, and by opposing end them." Only by *dying*, like the laughing rose, one may overcome the "sea of troubles." Hamlet perceives correctly that "dying" just may end all the heartache and shocks that ordinary life brings. Therefore, such "dying" is a solution that one may wish for. But Hamlet does not understand the meaning of "dying." Despite having an extraordinary intellectual ability, Hamlet is not able to figure out how to overcome the challenges associated with his struggle towards arriving at the stage "to be."

Unlike Hamlet, Khayaam may be able to escape from this sort of intellectual trap. His Guide provides him with a recipe, "But wine solves all enigmas that obtrude":

## 60

Eternity eternally discussed!
In hours of joy wine will not play us false.
Knowledge and practice lie beyond our scope
But wine solves all enigmas that obtrude.


The Guide's "In hours of joy" indicates that now is the right time for Khayaam to immerse himself completely in *drunkenness*. But he should "choose your vintage well." He has to *increase* the quality of his attention to the Guide's presence.

# Foes call me philosopher

Khayaam decides to forget about his debates about faith and reason. Instead, he follows the Guide's advice. He tries to switch his attention away from theology and logic and immerse himself in *drunkenness*:

## 61

I shall possess myself of a great goblet
With pipes of wine for its replenishment,
Annulling former ties to Faith and Reason
By marriage with this daughter of the Vine.

Shakespeare's Hamlet may help to grasp the meaning of this quatrain. Ophelia is a symbolic manifestation of "this daughter of the Vine." Like Khayaam, Hamlet could resolve his problem "by marriage" with Ophelia. However, Hamlet is not able to recognize Ophelia's function. He has allowed himself to be duped by the Ghost of his father. He confuses esoteric with exoteric.

Khayaam, on the other hand, has recognized the difference between common sense and the ecstasy of drunkenness:

## 62

As one familiar with all exoterics
Of being and not-being, who has plumbed
The abyss of shame, how can I greet as valid
Any condition short of drunkenness?

Khayaam refuses to call himself a philosopher, and in so doing issues a rebuke to those who try to reduce his writings to some sort of intellectual rendering:

## 63

Misguided foes call me philosopher -
God knows this is the one thing I am not.
I am even less: in such a nest of sorrows
I cannot tell you even who I am.

Khayaam starts to perceive that he is not yet in the position to tell "who I am." And those who consider him a sort of intellectual sceptic are simply misguided fools.

There is however an important factor that Khayaam has ignored. It is not enough that he himself gets "a great goblet with pipes of wine." In addition to the right *vintage* and the right *time*, there is also the requirement for the right *place* and the right *company*. The right company is needed if the *drinking* is to serve fully its function. In the following quatrain, Khayaam describes how he was provided with a hint about how to improve his drinking. Drinking alone and outside of the *tavern* does not lead to the needed outcome:

## 64

In drink this evening, as I passed the tavern,
A fellow toper met me with a flask.
Cried I: 'Old man, have you no awe of God?'
'Come', he said, 'God is bountiful! Come, drink!'

In this quatrain, the *tavern* indicates a travelers' meditation hall. Khayaam is told by a fellow toper that it is not enough to submerge oneself alone in the Guide's presence; he should join his *Friends* in the tavern.

# The Ninth Counsel: Banish your crowding griefs

Now the Guide describes the function of *drunkenness* by comparing it to "wine's alchemy":

### 65

Banish your crowding griefs with wine, disperse
Your memories of the two-and-seventy sects
And praise wine's alchemy that still can banish
With one red draught more than a thousand spites.

If one drinks at the right time and the right place with the right company, "wine's alchemy" can remove "more than a thousand spites."

It is said that man must develop by his own effort. This effort aims at an inner growth of an evolutionary nature that leads to the development of one's inner being. It may be compared to the alchemical process, where man's ordinary consciousness is transmuted into a permanent supracognitive perception. During the process, man's mind has to be focused on the supreme priority. The reference to "the two-and-seventy sects" emphasizes the challenges of keeping that focus fixed on the priority. The supreme priority is often referred to as One, i.e., Unity. The symbolic meaning of "seventy two" is "unity of multiplicity," it refers to various aspects and qualities that constitute *One*. Paying too much attention to one or a few randomly selected aspects would lead to disunity. The Guide warns Khayaam against following such an imbalanced approach.

## I have strayed this way and that

Khayaam declares that he has followed the previous advice and joined his Friends ("fellow-topers") in the tavern. He realizes that it is important to drinks in the right company:

66

I drink wine as my fellow-topers drink.
How much I drink can seem of small concern
To God, who knows well that I drink. Abstention
From drink would make God's knowledge ignorance.

Moralist and formal religionists are ignorant of the operation of the higher states of the mind. They tend to believe that spiritual advancement depends upon the cultivation of reward and punishment themes alone. It is them that now Khayyam addresses in the following quatrain. He says that in the state of drunkenness such concepts as Hellfire and God's Judgment Day take on a very different meaning. In the state of spiritual intoxication, there is no difference between yesterday and tomorrow, between "your Now and your Hereafter." In that state, one is capable to raise above all the worlds:

### 67

They say: 'Be sober, lest you die of drink
And earn Hellfire on God's Last Judgement Day.'
Nevertheless my blaze of drunkenness
Outshines both worlds: your Now and your Hereafter.

The following comment by Leonato in *Much Ado About Nothing* is Shakespeare's indication that philosophical debates are of no practical use as far as the evolutionary process is concerned:

For there was never yet philosopher
That could endure the toothache patiently,
However they have writ the style of gods,
And made a push at chance and sufferance.
(*Much Ado About Nothing, V.1*)

Noticing that enduring "the toothache" refers to being in love, i.e., being *intoxicated*, helps to grasp the meaning of Leonato's remark.

Khayaam reflects on his previous experiences. He realizes that, in the past, he has explored various schools of thought but he has not been able to meet anyone who found the way and then returned to help others:

### 68

My wandering feet have led me through far plains
And valleys: I have strayed this way and that
Yet never found a traveller who could boast
That he had ever trod the same road twice.

Hamlet comes to a similar observation in his famous soliloquy "To be, or not to be," evoking:

The undiscover'd country, from whose bourn
no traveller returns, ...
(*Hamlet, III.1*)

The term "The undiscover'd country" refers to the stage "to be." The guide is a "traveler" who has returned from "the undiscovered country," who has *died before dying,* and is capable of guiding others. Hamlet is still ignorant of the possibilities offered by "the undiscover'd country" and does not realize that travel to "the undiscover'd country" is the only solution to his problem. But he would need a guide who would show him the way. With the help of a guide, Hamlet would be able to free himself from the destructive influence of the Ghost. Such a guide is *present* in Elsinore, but Hamlet's arrogance has made him incapable of recognizing him.

Traditionally and historically, "exemplars of the cultured and genteel" refer to members of the royal families and aristocracy. Originally, this description was applied to those who were the Custodians of the evolutionary process. Khayaam indicates that contemporary "exemplars of the cultured and genteel," however, have lost this capacity:

69

Exemplars of the cultured and genteel
Though moulding candles from these predicates
Have never lighted one to mark the way
By night; but told their fables and slept on.

The term "the cultured and genteel" took on an artificial meaning. Presently, the members of "the cultured and genteel" do not have anything to do with being able to direct or even contribute to the process.

Shakespeare also indicated in his plays that the European royals had lost their role as those responsible for directing the evolutionary process. Such a transition of the leading role from the royals to a select group among the middle and lower classes is symbolically illustrated in *The Merry Wives of Windsor*.[29]

Khayaam realizes that his mind was impregnated with the desire to understand the purpose of his existence. His Guide gave him a hint that the key to the secret of existence ("Pen and Tablet, Heaven and Hell") lies in himself:

70

> Already at Creation I stretched out
> For Pen and Tablet, also Heaven and Hell;
> But prudently my Teacher warned me: 'Pen
> And Tablet, Heaven and Hell, lie in yourself.'

The Guide's hint is a reflection of the formula: "as above so below." In *Book IV* of the *Mathnawi*, Rumi explains the meaning of this formula. Namely, a more advanced structure serves as a matrix for a lower structure. The physical universe, the human body, the mind, spiritual matter, and spiritual essence consecutively represent substances in increasing degrees of refinement. The universe, with

---

[29] See Note #6.

its stars, galaxies and planets is the dwelling place of material substances. The human body is the dwelling place of the mind. The mind is the dwelling place of spiritual matter and of essence. In other words, the physical universe is a projection of the human mind. By developing his mind, man may free himself from the bonds of physical existence.

Consequently, Khayaam realizes that the world around him is just a reflection of his inner state, i.e., his hell and his paradise:

71

My broken body serves the Sky for girdle,
My precious tears carved out the Jihun's bed;
Hell is the furnace for my suffering soul;
Paradise, my one moment of release.

His suffering is caused by separation from his inner heart; his happiness are moments of *drunkenness*.

## The Tenth Counsel: Live in no awe of planets

The Guide explains that our ordinary perception of the world is just a shadow of reality. He compares it to a magic shadow-show being played on a screen illuminated by the sun. We all are like shadows endlessly rehearsing our phantom-like roles:

### 72

This vault, underneath which we live bemused
Is, so to speak, God's magic shadow-show:
With sun for lamp, the world as a wide screen
For countless lie-rehearsing silhouettes.

This world may be compared to the shadow and the next one to the sun. If you move towards your shadow (i.e., this world) it recedes and if pursued cannot be caught. If, however, you move towards the sun (the other world) your shadow will follow you.

This situation is alluded to by Prospero's speech in Shakespeare's *The Tempest*:

These our actors
(As I foretold you) were all spirits, and
Are melted into air, into thin air,
And like the baseless fabric of this vision,
The cloud-capp'd tow'rs, the gorgeous palaces,
The solemn temples, the great globe itself,
Yea, all which it inherit, shall dissolve,

And, like this insubstantial pageant faded
Leave not a rack behind. We are such stuff
As dreams are made on; and our little life
Is rounded with a sleep.
(*The Tempest*, IV.1)

Prospero explains the nature of the visible world. The visible world is perceived via the ordinary or physical senses. The physical senses belong to the ordinary or mortal state. Any sensation provided by the ordinary senses is a product of an undeveloped mind or an idle brain. According to Mercutio in *Romeo and Juliet*, dreams are the products of such an idle brain:

True, I talk of dreams,
Which are the children of an idle brain,
Begot of nothing but vain fantasy,
Which is as thin of substance as the air,
And more inconstant than the wind, ...
(*Romeo and Juliet, I.4*)

In other words, sensations within the visible world are a form of dreaming; the visible world is like a sleeper's dream and a sleeper's fancy. Consequently, undeveloped man is made of "such stuff as dreams are made on." For such undeveloped man, the entire world with its towers topped with clouds, its gorgeous palaces, solemn temples, the globe itself and everyone living in it - is just as illusory as a magic shadow-show.

Ordinary man is part of a puppet show. He is like a toy put on the table of existence and, after a short time, thrown back into non-existence. This applies to those who do not make a conscious effort to free themselves from total dependence on their raw ego:

73

> Let me speak out, unallegorically:
> We are mere puppets of our Master, toys
> On the Table of Existence, one by one
> Flung back in the toy box of Non-existence.

As long as we are being driven by our raw ego, we are like a ball struck by Fate's bat, running senselessly in all directions:

74

> Poor ball, struck by Fate's heavy polo-mallet,
> Running whichever way it drives you, numbed
> Of sense, though He who set you on your course,
> He knows, He knows, He knows.

Shakespeare's Pericles goes through similar experiences. He compares himself to a tennis-ball:

> A man whom both the water and the wind
> In that vast tennis-court, hath made the ball
> For them to play upon
> (*Pericles, Prince of Tyre, II.1*)

Those who are too much attached to the physical world have a fixed destiny. Their future is decided and their griefs and pains are irrelevant:

75

What we shall be is written, and we are so.
Heedless of Good or Evil, pen, write on!
By the first day all futures were decided;
Which gives our griefs and pains irrelevancy.

Consequently, evil and good, sorrow and joy are the predestined lot
of ordinary man. This is like the predestined orbits of planets.
Planets cannot change their paths. But man, through conscious
effort may change his destiny:

> The people of the world have a fixed destiny. But the
> spiritually developed receive what is *not* in their destiny.[30]

This is why the Guide tells Khayaam that the planets are much
"more impotent" than man. Therefore, "live in no awe of planets":

76

Evil and Good dispute the heart's possession;
Sorrow and Joy are man's predestined lot.
Live in no awe of planets. Planets are
One thousand times more impotent than we.

---

[30] *Recitals of the Saints*, Fariduddin Attar (quoted by Idries Shah in *Learning How to Learn*, Octagon Press, 1978).

This is what Edmund in Shakespeare's play *King Lear* has to say about the influence of planets:

> This is the excellent foppery of the world, that,
> when we are sick in fortune, often the surfeit
> of our own behavior, we make guilty of our
> disasters the sun, the moon, and the stars: as
> if we were villains by necessity; fools by
> heavenly compulsion; knaves, thieves, and
> treachers, by spherical predominance; drunkards,
> liars, and adulterers, by an enforced obedience of
> planetary influence; and all that we are evil in,
> by a divine thrusting on: an admirable evasion
> of whoremaster man, to lay his goatish
> disposition to the charge of a star!
> (*King Lear*, I.2)

Edmund says that it is simply a mark of stupidity that, when things go against us -often due to our own behaviour- we blame the sun, the moon, and the stars for disasters. Such an attitude implies that we are forced to be villains; that the heavens made us fools; the stars forced us to be knaves, thieves and traitors. We are only drunkards, liars, and adulterers because of the influence of the planets. We blame everything we do wrong on the influence of heaven: what a great excuse for these sluttish men to blame their randy nature on the stars!

By being influenced by grief and unconscious labor, man further conforms himself to an impotent destiny. Here is the Guide's sarcastic comment about Khayaam's distress:

## 77

Truth is hyperbole, my heart of hearts.
Why are you so distressed by grief and labour?
Yield to your destiny, conform, conform!
Tomorrow too is framed by destiny.

So, if you do not make a conscious effort to free yourself from your "inept desires," you may be comforted by the fact that your "tomorrow" has already been "mapped out for you":

## 78

Yesterday they determined your today
Exempt from yesterday's inept desires.
Rejoice that by no effort of your own
Tomorrow also is mapped out for you.

This train of thoughts is also illustrated by Shakespeare's in Macbeth's soliloquy:

To-morrow, and to-morrow, and to-morrow,
Creeps in this petty pace from day to day,
To the last syllable of recorded time;
And all our yesterdays have lighted fools
The way to dusty death. Out, out, brief candle!
Life's but a walking shadow, a poor player
That struts and frets his hour upon the stage,
And then is heard no more. It is a tale

Told by an idiot, full of sound and fury,
Signifying nothing.
(*Macbeth*, *V.5*)

Macbeth's soliloquy emphasizes the fact that ordinary life is
devoted to chasing after worldly desires. To the last moment of our
live ("To the last syllable of recorded time") we are preoccupied
with our tomorrow's egotistic objectives. We do not know how to
live, appreciate and use the *present*. In other words, we are like fools
who are wasting their lives on meaningless pursuits ("all our
yesterdays have lighted fools"). Macbeth realizes that he, like
Jaques in *As You Like It*, is just "a poor player ... upon the stage"
whose life became "a tale told by an idiot, full of sound and fury,
signifying nothing."

The Guide continues his explanations of how one may get hold of
the keys to the secret of existence that "lie in yourself." It was
already at the time of creation that our soul was made drunk with
immortal *wine* and a fragment of our *heart* was made into the keys
to Reality. Through the development of one's inner heart it is
possible to get hold of these *keys*:

79

But while the Eternal One created me
He word by word spelt out my lesson, love,
And seized my heart and from a fragment cut
Keys to the storehouse of Reality.

Man's life is a journey, a voyage. There is a point of birth and a
destiny. But between these two points a person is a free man.
Between these two points there is the journey, the search for the

hidden *keys*. It is this search, or traveling, that is important. People can travel and arrive at their destination empty-handed, or they can arrive with something which will benefit them in the place which they call their destiny.

# I shall have drunk

After digesting the Guide's previous counsel, Khayaam has finally understood the limitations of his ordinary intellect. In the following quatrains, he demonstrates the operation of reason and linear thinking patterns. Khayaam mimics the line of thoughts of intellectual hair-splitters. In their idle intellectual gymnastics, they attempt to prove that there is no need for an objective judgment of our actions. If everything is ordered by God, they say, how could we be responsible for our actions? When the world was created, our destiny was already determined. If our experiences are predetermined and we can't do anything about them, what is the purpose of life? Why then could it be even possible to make any errors?

80

When first the Sky's wild horses won their saddles,
When Jupiter first blazed, the Pleiads too,
My fate was published from God's Judgement seat.
How can I err? I act as it is written.

They sarcastically claim that the mysteries of creation can be more effectively resolved by disputing them in drunken company than by mumbling prayers:

## 81

Mysteries broached with joy in tavern talk
Have far more substance than a mumbled prayer
To you, my Last and First, my soul's Creator
Empowered either to sear or succour me.

By following reason, one may claim that whatever we do was precisely predetermined. Why should we then be faced with the Day of Judgement?

## 82

When, bending low, God moulded me from clay,
Incontrovertibly my life was ordered:
Without His order I abstain from crime.
Why should I burn, then, on His Judgement Day?

If the Creator prepared traps to catch us in our wrongdoing, why should we feel guilty of committing any misdeeds?

## 83

That sin is irresistible, He knows;
Yet He commands us to abstain from sin.
Thus irresistibility confounds us
With prohibition: - 'Lean, but never fall!'

How can we be blamed for what we are when all our actions have been predetermined by Him who fashioned us:

### 84

The clay from which this human frame was moulded
Forewarned a hundred wonders for me; yet -
Could I be worse or better than I am
Who was, even before He fashioned me?

If the Creator set snares on our every step, why should we even try to avoid them? If all things were apparently ordered by the Creator, would not any attempt of avoiding the snares be an act of rebellion against Him?

### 85

On every path I take, Your snares are spread
To entrap me, should I walk without due care.
Utter extremes acknowledge Your vast sway.
You order all things - yet You call me rebel?

Khayaam continues mimicking the arguments of his erudite colleagues and asks how mercy fits into this equation. It is obvious that obedience is required and good deeds are to be rewarded. But what about mercy? When are God's mercy and grace to be applied?

## 86

If sinfully I drudge, where is Your mercy?
If clouds darken my heart, where is Your light?
Heaven rewards my practice of obedience;
Rewards well-earned are good - but what of grace?

God is able to punish all. Yet, God is also able to forgive all. Why does not God grant us His mercy? Or at least bestow on us repentance, so we may avoid His punishment?

## 87

You, always cognisant of every secret;
Who succour all flesh in its hour of need,
Grant me repentance, grant me mercy too -
You who forgive all, You who punish all,

After all God is our Master; God has created us. Who then is responsible for our errors? Did God not sin by creating sinners?

## 88

Ordaining every cause for life or death,
Guarding this tattered robe we call the Sky,
Say, am I sinful? Are you not my Master?
Who sins when You alone created me?

At this point it is interesting to see how Portia in Shakespeare's *The Merchant of Venice* explains the operation of God's mercy:

> The quality of mercy is not strain'd,
> It droppeth as the gentle rain from heaven
> Upon the place beneath. It is twice blest:
> It blesseth him that gives and him that takes.
> 'Tis mightiest in the mightiest, it becomes
> The throned monarch better than his crown.
> His sceptre shows the force of temporal power,
> The attribute to awe and majesty,
> Wherein doth sit the dread and fear of kings;
> But mercy is above this sceptred sway,
> It is enthroned in the hearts of kings,
> It is an attribute to God himself;
> And earthly power doth then show likest God's
> When mercy seasons justice. ...
> (*The Merchant of Venice, IV.1*)

Portia says that *mercy* is not something that can be enforced or demanded. Yet, *mercy* covers everyone and everything; it drops like soft rain from heaven. It is an attribute to God himself. *Mercy* is always present. Even though ordinary man is incapable of perceiving it, the fact that he is able to question the existence of God is a manifestation of God's mercy.

In the following quatrains, Khayaam extends his mimicking of his erudite colleagues by comparing them to "pots" who are trying to reason out the purpose of their existence by asking: Who is the Potter? Who is the salesman? Who is the customer? Khayaam uses this image to demonstrate the irrelevancy of linear thinking patterns:

## 89

I saw at least two thousand pots, last night
In Potters Row, not all of which were mute,
And one cried loudly: 'Friends, where is the Potter,
Where is the salesman, where the customer?'

Such linear thinking patterns can only lead to winning a debate and
to short-lived satisfaction but they do not remove doubts nor cause
certainty. Only through experience may one arrive at a state that
puts the mind at rest in serenity:

Knowledge without serenity
Is an unlit candle;
together they are honey-comb;
honey without wax is a noble thing;
wax without honey is only fit for burning.[31]

Khayaam has arrived at the state where he realizes that his
understanding may only be advanced by the right action at the right
time. Symbolically, such conditions are represented by the month
of Ramazan. In the following quatrain, he indicates that the new
moon marking Ramazan is fast approaching:

[31] *The Walled Garden of Truth*, Hakim Sanai (see Note #24).

## 90

Ramazan's moon, I hear, rides high again,
Soon none may give new rein to hot desire;
Yet before Shaban ends, I shall have drunk
Sweet wine enough to float me through that Fast.


Khayaam puts aside his relentless questioning and prepares himself, as best as he can, so he may be ready for the coming experience of *dying* to earthly attachments.

## The Eleventh Counsel: Yet never fear

The Guide picks up Khayaam's image of the bowls as the representation of mankind to deliver his next counsel. In this counsel, the Guide prepares Khayaam for the experience of death. He uses the term "one bowl praised by the wide wise world" to describe the function of the Guide of the Age. The Guide of the Age serves as a living exemplar, or a matrix, for the entire evolutionary process of humanity. A rather surprising or even shocking function of the Guide of the Age is his role in sustaining humanity. Namely, the whole human community only continues to exist in physical form because of the work and the life of the Guide of the Age. Here is an explanation given to Shakespeare by his mentor:

> Herein lives wisdom, beauty, and increase,
> Without this, folly, age, and cold decay.
> If all were minded so, the times should cease,
> And threescore year would make the world away.
> (*Sonnet 11*)

Shakespeare's mentor tells him that within man there is a seed of knowledge, beauty, and growth ("Herein lives wisdom, beauty, and increase"). Without this seed, there would be only ignorance, destruction, and death ("Without this folly, age, and cold decay"). If none would be taking care of the seed, then time would end and the entire world would collapse within the life-time of a man ("If all were minded so, the times should cease,/And threescore year would make the world away").

A similar explanation of the role of the Guide of the Age was provided by Rumi:

If the Guide of the Age would vanish, destiny would come
upon us and the entire world would collapse.
(*Mathnawi, Book I*)

During his life, such an individual has to perform the work which
will be done eventually through the following generations. Yet, says
the Guide, even this "bowl praised by the wide wise world" is not
immune to destruction; the greatest exemplar of humanity has also
to taste death:

### 91

There is one bowl praised by the wide wise world
That tempts a toper to a hundred kisses;
And yet the Potter moulds this fragile clay
Only to fall and shatter on the ground.

The Guide recalls Khayaam's previous thoughts about the
seemingly senseless fate of human life:

### 92

The elements that constitute a bowl
Hate all besotted murderers of bowls -
Bowls deftly moulded for the love of whom?
Then dashed to pieces, as a curse on whom?

The Guide points out that by following this sort of argument, one could spend one's entire life trying to figure out what the purpose of life is. And at the end, one will not be able to satisfy oneself and most probably will arrive at the conclusion that there is no hope at all if even the best exemplar of humankind cannot avoid death:

93

Our Guardian chose our natures. Is He then
Delinquent when He treats us with disorder?
We ask: 'Why break the best of us?' and murmur:
'Is the pot guilty if it stands awry?'

The "bowls" are but containers. The container is skillfully made so it can store life's essence. Therefore, the container is irrelevant. At one point it is discarded, so the essence may be released. This is why even a Perfect Man has to taste death. Before he dies, his function is transferred -like Abdul-Qadir's "patched robe"- to a successor. It is in this way that humanity is sustained.

Being preoccupied with worldly matters does not allow one to grasp the meaning of life. The Guide brings in an orthodox view of God as "a short-tempered Judge" to point out that such a simplified view marks an ignorance that functions as a veil preventing one from understanding the overall modus operandi of the formula: "Nothing of Evil can proceed from Good":

## 94

Though Judgement Day should prove a grand ordeal
Handled, they say, by a short-tempered Judge,
Yet never fear: Good has the final word -
Nothing of Evil can proceed from Good.


It is this formula that may help one to arrive at the knowledge of man's place in the Universe and the nature of that Universe. This is the only knowledge that can make man free and allow him to progress toward a higher form of life.

The Guide's words "Yet never fear: good has the final word" signals that, during the month of Ramazan, Khayaam concluded his earthly phase of the journey. Now he is ready to depart.

# Remould me as a jug

After listening to the Guide's previous counsel, Khayaam is preparing himself for his physical death. He knows that his experiences may benefit others. By benefitting others, he himself may be revived. Therefore, he expresses a wish to be remolded as a jug "well soused in glorious drink," i.e., as a container well soaked in *divine essence*:

## 95

When this existence finds an end at last,
When all I am scatters to the four winds,
Let them remould me as a jug, that then
I may revive, well soused in glorious drink.

Khayaam appeals to his friends to "contrive" such a jug. In this way he will be able to help them:

## 96

When Destiny, I say, has trod me down
Cutting my root of hope, sweet friends, assemble
And from my clay contrive a single jug
To thrive again, well soused in glorious drink.

The end of Ramazan marked the end of the forceful occasion. Khayaam readies himself to celebrate the earthly phase of his journey:


### 97

Shawal is with us, Ramazan has passed.
Salute the month of joy and lutes and singing.
When wineskins for the shoulder cry aloud:
'Here come the porters, one after another!'


Khayaam knows that his "dry corpse will be no treasure trove." Therefore, he instructs his friends on how they may remold him into a jug "well soused in glorious drink." Namely, they should ignore all his faults ("wash me in wine") and focus their attention on his writings:


### 98

Should I fall dead, wash my poor corpse in wine;
Read it into the grave with drinking songs.
On Judgement Day, if you have need of me,
Delve in the soil beneath our tavern door.


His poems contain the *essence* of his experiences. It is this *essence* that will guide them towards the fulfilment of their heart desire.

A similar instruction was attached to the *First Folio*, the first collection of Shakespeare's plays printed in 1623. The instruction emphasized the importance of the inner content of Shakespeare's plays and their function as a guiding tool. The instruction said:

> Read him, therefore, and again, and again. And if then you do not like him, surely you are in some manifest danger, not to understand him. And so we leave you to other of his Friends, whom if you need, can be your guides: if you need them not, you can lead yourself, and others. And such Readers we wish him.[32]

Just like in the case of Khayaam's poetry, the inner meaning of Shakespeare's plays may be fully grasped when *digesting* them with the help of "Friends."

Khayaam advises his friends that they should gather together in the tavern and read his poems. His poems serve as a container ("coffin-wood") which preserves the *essence* of his experiences:

### 99

> Take heed to pamper me with bowls that change
> A pasty-coloured cheek to ruby red.
> When I fall dead, I say, wash me in wine
> And use the vine's own slats for coffin-wood.

The impact of Khayaam's experiences is like "the wine's bouquet." It will help seekers after truth navigate their steps during their spiritual *drunkenness*:

---

[32] *To the great Variety of Readers* by John Heminge and Henrie Condell (*First Folio*, 1623).

## 100

So lovingly I drink, the wine's bouquet
Will scent the air where I lie underground;
A toper treading past my grave will pause
To sniff, and find himself ignobly drunk.

Khayaam remarks that prayers and fasting did not help him in experiencing the divine scent. Instead, he was set free by a sip of *wine*:

## 101

Once, years ago, inclined to prayer and fasting
I swore my soul was free and given to God.
Alas for purity once more besmirched -
For a vow broken by one sip of wine!

Some 250 years later, Khayaam's remark was repeated by Hafiz:

With wine, with red wine your prayer carpet dye![33]

Khayaam has consciously abandoned his professional career. He is aware that his actions and his poems have ruined his reputation as a scientist and a scholar. Yet, he says, there is nothing in this world that he values as much as *wine*:

---

[33] *Teaching of Hafiz*, translated by Gertrude Bell (Octagon Press, 1979).

## 102

Though drink has rotted my high reputation,
Reject it I will not, while I yet breathe,
Wondering often what the vinters buy
Equal in value with the wine they sell.

The fact that Khayaam's reputation was rotten is consistent with Rumi's advice:

Know that reputation is of a great hindrance in the path.
(*Divan-e Shams-e Tabrizi*[34])

Khayaam has effectively managed to *die* to his worldly ambitions and pride. After *dying* to his worldly attachments, he is well prepared to depart from this world. He is surprised at how brief his earthly life was:

## 103

Ah me, the book of early glory closes,
The green of Spring makes way for wintry snow.
The cheerful bird of Youth flutters away -
I hardly noticed how it came or went.

The remaining part of his life seems to him to be too long. He realizes that he could have achieved much more than he did. He

---

34 See Note #7.

wonders if his deeds are sufficient enough for his *essence* to resurface in the form of scented flowers:

### 104

If only I could find some tranquil spot
For sleep; if only this long road would end!
If only from some inner core of earth
We might spring up once more to bud and blossom!

Saadi of Shiraz used a similar allegory to explain the transmuting effect of *essence*. He says that one day he came upon a piece of perfumed clay. Intoxicated by its fragrance he asked:

"Are you musk or ambergris?"
The clay replied
"I am but a bit
of worthless clay but I have
associated with a rose.
Thus the virtue of my companion
had effect upon me though I am
the clay I always was."[35]

In the following quatrain, Khayaam expresses a wish that the world were designed in such a way that not just a few but all souls could be fully satisfied with their hearts' desire:

---

[35] *The Rose Garden*, Saadi (translated by Omar Ali-Shah, Tractus Books, 1997).

## 105

If only I controlled God's Universe,
Would I not wipe away these faulty Heavens
And build from nothing a true Paradise
Where all souls could achieve their hearts' desire?

Khayaam's sentimental wish prompts the Guide to deliver his last counsel.

## The Twelfth Counsel: Content yourself

In his last counsel, the Guide refers to Khayaam's latest wish of "a true Paradise, where all souls could achieve their hearts' desire." The Guide tells him that he should not be concerned with the future or other peoples' fate. Instead, he should be content with what he has experienced so far. The Guide points towards the tombs of previous travelers ("bowls emptied by moonlight") and tells Khayaam that thanks to their efforts the world has been sustained. The Guide compares himself to the Sun by addressing Khayaam as "my mortal Moon." Then he adds that, one day, they both will join the previous travellers, "the Moon may search the world for us, but find us gone":

### 106

> Since no voice here can promise you tomorrow,
> Content yourself, my mortal Moon, with bowls
> Emptied by moonlight - one fine night the Moon
> May search the world for us, but find us gone!

The Guide's counsel parallels the advice given by Abdul-Qadir to his disciples, "You shall be rewarded; and they shall have the reward of their efforts and of your aspiration."

Now the Guide addresses Khayaam's friends. He announces that he and Khayaam will be departing. But his friends should keep Khayaam in their memories. When the next time they join together

in a drinking session, they should turn down Khayaam's empty
bowl as an act of gratitude to their former companion:


107

Sweet friends, in joy assembled here together,
Never forget us, once your sweetest friends.
Before you greet the jug, Khayaam adjures you:
When his turn comes, turn down his empty bowl.


In the following quatrain, the Guide reaffirms that Khayaam, the
Tentmaker, dedicated his life to stitching "the hides for Wisdom's
tent." And he advises Khayaam's friends, saying that they should
not destroy his achievements with their grief. By grieving Khayaam,
they would be misusing him; they would be giving themselves idly
up to death:


108

Khayaam, who stitched the hides for Wisdom's tent
Has tumbled in Grief's clutches. He lies burning;
The shears of Death have closed upon his guys
And Hope the Broker sells him for a song.


Those who grieve Khayaam's death are fools who deserve "the
eternal fires of Hell." How do they dare, asks the Guide, to plead
for Omar's pardon? Previously they scorned at God's mercy, but
now they are shamelessly "Nudging his mercy from the Merciful":

109

Fools, with damnation as your destiny,
Sentenced to fuel the eternal fires of Hell,
How long will you still plead for Omar's pardon,
Nudging his mercy from the Merciful?

In the above quatrain, the Guide addresses the Poet not as Khayaam but as Omar. Omar is a New Man. In this way, the Guide points out that through the process illustrated in the previous quatrains, *Khayaam* was transmuted into *Omar*. In other words, by correctly discharging his undertaking of "stitching the hides for Wisdom's tent," the Poet *died* to his ordinary self and arrived at the stage of permanent life. He was able to overcome death. Shakespeare alluded to this type of experience in *Sonnet 146*:

So shall thou feed on Death, that feeds on men,
And Death once dead, there's no more dying then.
(*Sonnet 146*)

An identical line of thought may be found in Rumi's *Mathnawi*:

Let the body fade away while the inner being accumulates true riches. In this way, the inner being may be fed on death, while death is fed on ordinary men.
(*Mathnawi, Book II*)

Here are Rumi's comments explaining further this form of death and rebirth:

130

From his present state, man needs to continue his migration so that he may escape from his rationality and intellectuality which are driven mostly by greed and egotism. There are a hundred thousand more marvellous states ahead of him. He fell asleep and became oblivious of the past. This world is the sleeper's dream and the sleeper's fancies. Till all of a sudden there shall rise the dawn of death and he shall be delivered from ignorance.
(*Mathnawi, Book IV*)

I died to my selfish self once and for all; then I came back to a new life. I tasted the bitterness of death and non-existence. After such an experience only a fool would go back to his previous life.
(*Mathnawi, Book V*)

O you who possess sincerity, if you want that Reality unveiled, choose death and tear off the veil. Not such a death that you will go into a grave, but a death consisting of inner transformation, so that you will be able to see a Light.
(*Mathnawi, Book VI*)

Shakespeare disclosed details about himself and his background in his plays by using a similar symbolic transmutation to that of *Khayyam* and *Omar*. He chose *William Page* as a character that represented him. His personal progress along the path is symbolically indicated as the transmutation of *Robin, a Page*, into *William Page* - who appears in *The Merry Wives of Windsor*, the second last play of Shakespeare's narrative.[36]

In accordance with Rumi's counsel, this form of transmutation marks the arrival at the stage of certainty:

---

[36] See Note #6.

In this context, materialistic knowledge is above opinion, but is inferior to certainty. Only through reaching a stage of certainty can man escape from the pangs of death and time.
(*Mathnawi, Book III*)

Deaths and rebirths are experiences that a spiritual traveler is going through during the various stages of his evolutionary growth.

## Yet will I not despair of mercy

The Poet declares that, since he has become *Omar*, he has experienced *unity*. It is the *unity* of aspects and qualities addressed by the Guide in the quatrain #65. Now he is able to say that he will not despair of mercy because he did not argue that "the One was Two":

### 110

> Though pearls in praise of God I never strung,
> Though dust of sin lies clotted on my brow,
> Yet will I not despair of mercy. When
> Did Omar argue that the One was Two?

Omar has arrived at the stage where God's curtain mentioned by the Guide in his Fifth Counsel was removed and "we two" became "one" (the quatrain #35). This experience is explained by Rumi in the following story:

One went to the door of the Beloved and knocked. A voice asked:
"Who is there?"
He answered: "It is I."
The voice said: "There is no room here for me and thee." The door was shut.

After a year of solitude and depravation this man returned to the door of the Beloved. He knocked. A voice from within asked:

"Who is there?" The man said:

"It is Thou."

The door was opened for him.[37]

It is in this context that one should be beware of the word "two":

> Is it you or I,
>> This reality in the eye?
> Beware, beware
>> Of the word "two"![38]

The quatrain #110 is Omar's self-epitaph. Omar announces that, prior to his physical death, he was able to abandon his *tent* and enter into the *room* of the Beloved.

---

[37] *The Way of the Sufi*, Idries Shah (Octagon Press, 1968).

[38] *Divine Flashes*, Fakhruddin 'Iraqi (see Note #15).

# The Vacant Palace

The quatrain #111 is the concluding stanza of *The Authentic Rubaiyyat*. It refers to "the fine night" mentioned in the quatrain #106, when "the Moon may search the world for us, but find us gone." "The palace with huge walls soaring to Heaven" is now vacant:

### 111

> The palace with huge walls soaring to Heaven,
> Where prostrate Kings did reverence at the gate -
> A ring-dove perches on its battlements;
> 'Where, where?' it coos, 'where, where?'

The palace with huge walls soaring to Heaven is a symbolic bridge connecting this world with other worlds. It was at the gate to this bridge that future Kings, i.e., successful travelers, "most perfect of our kind," were starting their journey. But now the palace is vacant. This is in accordance with Rumi's observation:

Of dervishes in this world, are left but ashes.
(*Mathnawi, Book I*)

The palace is an allegorical description of the human mind. In the *abjad* system, the number 111 signifies the vacant "palace" or the *mind* emptied from ordinary thoughts into which higher perception descends. This refers to those "most perfect of our kind" who were able to mount "the soaring Burak of their thought" and experience higher worlds (see the quatrain #27). This meaning is further emphasized in this quatrain by the appearance of a ring-dove that symbolizes the source of supracognitive perception. The *dove* is a reference to the traditions of Mohammed. Mohammed had a dove, which he used to feed with wheat out of his ear. When hungry, the dove would alight on his shoulder and thrust its bill in to find its food. This was a symbolic illustration of Mohammed's source of inspiration. Shakespeare alluded to this tradition by inserting the following comment by Charles, the Dauphin of France, in his conversation with Joan of Arc:

> Was Mahomet inspired with a dove?
> (*Henry VI, Part 1, I.2*)

The appearance of the ring-dove in the concluding quatrain of *The Authentic Rubaiyyat* marks the completion of the Poet's earthly journey. Like the Saki in the legend, the Poet has completed his *fortieth morning* of service. He purified his mind, i.e., he *died* to his earthly attachments. At this point he is presented with a cup of the Drink of the Immortals.

# CONCLUSION

As man follows the spiritual path, he goes through several stages. These stages are referred to as *deaths* and *rebirths*. Each death refers to overcoming certain automatic reactions and emotional reflexes; each rebirth marks the activation of a new subtle faculty of the mind. Man is to experience these stages before his physical death. In *The Rubaiyyat*, Khayaam emphasizes the experiences associated with the *first death*, the death of his linear thinking patterns.

Khayaam's method was to draw attention to the limitations of the intellectual and scholastic methods. He also advocates that everyone should make conscious efforts to refine oneself. Furthermore, Khayaam indicates that the promised *heaven* is available to man during his lifetime. An important thing to notice is that there is no *lover* in Khayaam's quatrains. The main theme of Khayaam's poetry is *drunkenness*. He emphasizes an early stage of the process, i.e., the purification of the ordinary intellect. Just as described by Falstaff, this is done by removing "all the foolish and dull and curdy vapours which environ it." Only after overcoming this conditioning, is it possible to activate a subtle faculty of the intellect; a new faculty is born. Khayaam indicated that his companions were not capable of overcoming the limitations of the ordinary intellect.

Rumi dedicated his writings to the next phase of the evolutionary process. Namely, Rumi's poetry is focused on the struggle with ordinary emotional and sentimental conditioning. Rumi illustrates these experiences as that of a lover who is separated from his beloved. The lover may be united with his bellowed only when his emotional attachments are consumed by the flames of *love*. This is referred to as the *second death*. This death has to be experienced before a subtle faculty of the heart may be activated. Rumi pointed out that, at that time, members of his community were not ready yet for this particular experience.

Shakespeare's plays illustrate a spiritual methodology that aims at the simultaneous activation of the subtle faculties of the intellect and the heart. This is why in Shakespeare's narrative there are four couples of lovers who struggle to be united at the same place and at the same time. However, Shakespeare indicated that 16th century man was incapable of experiencing fully such a union. In the concluding episode of his narrative, the lovers' *hearts* are artificially patched so they can partially experience a taste of the elevating union.[39] However, such a patched union could not last for too long. But this experience was needed to awaken an inner hunger that had a lasting effect, even for a long time after the disintegration of the union. It was this inner hunger that induced a thirst for some unknown but important knowledge. In this way, 16th century European man was encouraged to move forward and get closer to the discovery of his evolutionary purpose.

The writings of Khayaam, Rumi and Shakespeare comply with the general rule of the spiritual methodology which states that only by struggling towards a higher stage, a lower stage may be fully integrated. Therefore, a new evolutionary potentiality is made available to man while he is still struggling to come to terms with the previous ones. The question may be asked: what is the evolutionary potentiality applicable to us at the present time? If the writings of Khayaam, Rumi and Shakespeare are an indicative of three milestones on man's evolutionary path, what would be required from a man who finds himself living in the 21st century? Based on the methodology outlined in *The Authentic Rubaiyyat*, one would expect that the current phase of the process would aim at a fourth stage where the traveler is able to overcome the limitations of physical existence, i.e., when he is capable of turning his earthly attachments into *ashes*.

---

[39] See Note #6.

This fourth point along the curve representing human progress towards its evolutionary purpose is symbolically alluded to in a poem written by Omar Ali-Shah, the translator of *The Authentic Rubaiyyat*. It is a short poem that refers to the current stage of the process. It is a stage that transcends the worldly forms that were referred to at the previous stages, i.e., time, place, existence. At this stage there is no need for either wine or a beautiful girl. The aim of human conscious efforts has been moved up by another notch on the evolutionary ladder:

> I let go of my life
> in the hope of knowing You
> I let go of my life'
> but I can become
> the dust of your garden
> I will not drink the wine
> offered by a beautiful girl
>
> I have no need to drink the wine
> offered by a beautiful girl
> I have no need of that intoxication
> my intoxication is to be
> the dust in your garden
>
> On the morning of the day of reckoning
> when I lift my head from the grave
> I lift it to search for you
> I lift it to speak with you.[40]

This poem points towards the continuation of the spiritual experiences that were illustrated in Khayaam's, Rumi's and Shakespeare's poetry. The poem is a reference to a fourth stage when a new man is reborn from his ashes ("to live and love"). It is a challenging task. In order to comply with the current evolutionary

---

[40] *The Course of the Seeker*, Omar Ali-Shah (Tractus Books, 1996).

needs, 21st century man would be required to abandon his intellectual and emotional conditioning as the prime forces of his actions. Only then, a new organ of supracognitive perception can be temporarily switched on. This organ of perception would allow him to overcome, at least temporarily, the limitations of ordinary physical existence. It is in this context that Omar Ali-Shah's poem may serve as conclusion to our journey with Omar Khayaam.

# TROUBADOUR PUBLICATIONS

*Shakespeare's Elephant in Darkest England*, W. Jamroz (2016)

*Shakespeare's Sequel to Rumi's Teaching*, W. Jamroz (2015)

*Shakespeare's Sonnets or How heavy do I journey on the way*, W. Jamroz (2014)

*Shakespeare for the Seeker*, Volume 4, W. Jamroz (2013)

*Shakespeare for the Seeker*, Volume 3, W. Jamroz (2013)

*Shakespeare for the Seeker*, Volume 2, W. Jamroz (2013)

*Shakespeare for the Seeker*, Volume 1, W. Jamroz (2012)

www.ingramcontent.com/pod-product-compliance
Lightning Source LLC
Chambersburg PA
CBHW070812100426
42742CB00012B/2340